THE DRAMA OF
# LIVING

# THE DRAMA OF
# LIVING

*Becoming Wise in the Spirit*

## DAVID F. FORD

**BrazosPress**

*a division of Baker Publishing Group*
Grand Rapids, Michigan

Published by Brazos Press
a division of Baker Publishing Group
P.O. Box 6287, Grand Rapids, MI 49516-6287
www.brazospress.com

Printed in the United States of America

Library of Congress Cataloging-in-Publication Data
Ford, David, 1948–
    The drama of living : becoming wise in the spirit / David F. Ford.
        pages cm
    Includes bibliographical references and index.
    ISBN 978-1-58743-324-5 (pbk.)
    1. Christian life. 2. Christianity and culture. 3. Christianity—21st century.
    I. Title.
    BV4501.3F6435 2014
    248.4—dc23                                                      2014018136

14  15  16  17  18  19  20        7  6  5  4  3  2  1

In keeping with biblical principles of creation stewardship, Baker Publishing Group advocates the responsible use of our natural resources. As a member of the Green Press Initiative, our company uses recycled paper when possible. The text paper of this book is composed in part of post-consumer waste.

To Micheal, friend of friends
*Made, broken, and remade in love*

# Contents

Acknowledgments   ix

Introduction   xiii


1. The Drama of Living: Public and Ordinary   1

2. Improvising Wisdom: Within and between
   Traditions   25

3. Face-to-Face: The Heart of Life's Drama   49

4. Rereading and Rehearsing: Classic Surprises   77

5. Loving: Intimate, Dramatic, Ultimate   103

6. Improvised Lives: Timing, Aging, Dying   137

7. Playing without End: Wise in the Spirit   175


Appendix: A Vocation of Love   199

Notes   211

# Acknowledgments

There is a good deal of autobiography in this book, so the debts of gratitude are to most of the people who have been formative in my life from childhood onward. I cannot name them all, but some are especially relevant to the leading themes of the book.

The High School, Dublin, was my introduction to drama through Shakespeare, classics, and acting in school plays. Especially important were the Greek plays (performed in Greek!), both tragedy and comedy, that were produced annually by the headmaster, Dr. Ralph Reynolds, who also inspired a lifetime's interest in classics, the subject of my first degree at Trinity College Dublin. The superb department there included W. B. Stanford, Donald Wormell, Herbert Parkes, and John V. Luce. The tragedies of Sophocles made the strongest impression on me, but appreciation of "the drama of living" was also shaped by Homer's *Iliad* and *Odyssey*, Herodotus and Thucydides, Aeschylus and Euripides, Socrates and Plato, Horace, Catullus, Ovid, Cicero, Virgil, Juvenal, Plautus, and Tacitus.

Having gone on to study theology and religious studies, I have often been grateful for this immersion in Greek and Roman civilizations, worlds of meaning hardly affected (in the periods covered by my courses) by the Abrahamic traditions that became principal concerns in later life. Something of the combination of strangeness, richness, and (at the cost of some hard work) accessibility has been transferable to intercultural and interfaith engagement today.

Perhaps the most profound encounter with drama was in the conversations with and writings of one of my doctoral supervisors, Donald MacKinnon. In his own words, he "wrestled with reality at its darkest points" and brought Greek and Shakespearean tragedy, the crucifixion of Jesus, and the Holocaust into probing, disturbing, and anguished engagement with each other. He speculated what Christian theology would have been like if in its formative centuries it had paid more attention to the tragedies of Aeschylus, Sophocles, and Euripides than to the philosophies of the Stoics, Plato, and Aristotle. In a little, indirect way, the "dramatic" take on the Gospel of John in this book is doing that.

I owe to Murray Cox and his coauthor, Alice Theilgaard (see chapter 6), a very different approach to Shakespeare through psychotherapy and neurology and also an appreciation of the work of Mark Rylance, not least in bringing Shakespeare to Broadmoor. I am also indebted to Ben Quash on drama and theology, to Sam Wells on improvisation, and to Giles Waller on Luther and tragedy.

As I began researching and thinking about a theological commentary on the Gospel of John, there was a six-month period during which I had twenty-one three-hour sessions, one on each chapter of the Gospel, with two ideal fellow readers, Richard Hays and Richard Bauckham. In addition, many others have studied or discussed John with me, including those students in the Faculty of Divinity in Cambridge who have taken the final year course on John. It is mostly impossible to say what I have learned from whom, but such joint study has been immensely important both in interpreting specific passages and in shaping an overall approach. The practice of Scriptural Reasoning is a principal theme of chapter 2 and also figures in other chapters. It has been one of the formative influences in my life since writing *The Shape of Living*, and I am most grateful to all those who have helped in various ways to develop or sponsor the practice, including Ahmad Achtar, Nick Adams, Adam Afterman, Rumi Ahmed, Abdulrahman Al Salmi, Zainab Balogun, Barbara Bennett, Hanoch Ben-Pazi, Ayesha Chaudhry, Frances Clemson, Aryeh Cohen, Maria Dakake, Lejla Demiri, Miriam Feldmann-Kaye, Jennifer Fields, Emily Filler, Gavin Flood, Jim Fodor, David Frankel, Robert Gibbs, Tom Greggs, Usama Hasan, Hannah Hashkes, Rim Hassen, Mike Higton, Annabel Keeler, Steven Kepnes, Basit Koshul, Natan Levy, Miriam Lorie, Hilary Marlow, Yasmine Mermer, Rachel Muers, Aref Nayed, Peter Ochs, Chad Pecknold, Ben Quash, Randi Rashkover, Reuben Shank, Stephen Shashoua, Sarah Snyder, Laura Solomons, Sir Sigmund Sternberg, Lindsey Taylor-Guthartz, Susannah Ticciati, Muhammad Suheyl Umar, Isra Umeyye, Nargis Virani, Daniel Weiss, Tim Winter, Yang Huilin, You Bin, Simeon Zahl, and Laurie Zoloth.

The L'Arche communities are a theme of chapter 3 and also occur elsewhere. Since I was introduced to them more than twenty years ago by Frances Young, they have been a constant source of wisdom and prophetic challenge. On the international side, I thank Jean Vanier, Christine McGrievy, Jean-Christophe Pascal, Patrick Fontaine, Eileen Glass, George Durner, the participants from many countries in the retreat described in chapter 3, and many in Trosly-Breuil. Within the UK, I thank Michael Banner, John Bell, Christopher Bemrose, Rosemary Boyle, Hazel Bradley, Helen Brough, Ben Brown, Jude Brown, Stephen Conway, Clare Gardom, James Gardom, Judith Gardom, Lorraine Gelsthorpe, Katharine Hall, Lal Keenan, Anthony Kramers,

Patrick McKearney, Mark Molloy, Ian Randall, Janice Randall, John Sargent, John Simpson, Sarah Simpson, Sue Simpson, Margie Tolstoy, Thérèse Vanier, Rowan Williams, Hilary Wilson, and the first members of Lyn's House in Cambridge, initiated by Deborah, my wife: Giulia Conto, Heather Leppard, Matthew Harbage, and Justin Youngchan Choi.

Deborah became associate priest at St. James, Wulfstan Way, in Cambridge shortly after this book was begun. Settling into this new parish community has been a very good experience for both of us and an encouraging example of the drama of ordinary Christian living. The weekly Eucharist at the center of its parish life could have been a lens for a good deal in the book.

My greatest single debt is to Micheal O'Siadhail, not only for his poetry, which runs through this book, but also for discussions of each chapter and, above all, his friendship. The book is dedicated to him.

Others, too, have read all or parts of the book and made helpful comments, and I thank them: my wife, Deborah, and my children, Rebecca, Rachel, and Daniel; Jeremy Begbie, Jutta Brueck, Richard Chartres, Derek Fraser, Alan Hargrave, Annie Hargrave, Robbie Leigh, Christine McGrievy, Madeleine O'Callaghan, Jean-Christophe Pascal, Claire Salmon, Martin Seeley, Margie Tolstoy, the Worster family, and Jean Vanier.

Natalie Watson of SCM and Bob Hosack and Lisa Ann Cockrel of Brazos Press have been exemplary editors, and Frances Clemson has been a superb research associate.

# Introduction

This book has been a joy to write as well as a labor of love. It has drawn me deeper into the Bible, into Micheal O'Siadhail's poetry, and into life. The interplay of the three has led to rediscoveries, surprises, and fresh insights. My hope is that it might do something similar for readers who are seeking resources and inspiration for their roles in the drama of living.

This book is a sequel to *The Shape of Living*, which was an experiment, with a view to wiser living, drawing on the same combination of classic writings, accessible poetry, and contemporary life. The present book takes that further. It focuses on one biblical text, the Gospel of John, and reads it in relation to some core themes: public and ordinary dramas of living (chapter 1); learning wisdom in our pluralistic world (chapter 2); the centrality of face-to-face relationships (chapter 3); practices of rereading and rehearsing, and the habits that shape our lives (chapter 4); friendship, sex, God, and other aspects of love (chapter 5); how we cope with time, illness, aging, and dying (chapter 6); and O'Siadhail's "Madam Jazz" (chapter 7).

The same themes are taken up through the collections of poetry O'Siadhail has published in the fifteen years since *The*

*Shape of Living. Our Double Time* has especially contributed on time, dying, jazz, and friendship. *The Gossamer Wall: Poems in Witness to the Holocaust* has helped to reflect on the public drama of history and its traumas. *Love Life* has been central to the face-to-face and the concern with love throughout the book. *Globe* has given a broad, dramatic portrayal of our contemporary world, engaging with the dynamics of change, traumas and their aftermath, characters who have shaped our history, and the imagery of jazz—culminating in "Only End," which inspires the whole of chapter 7. *Tongues* has shaped the understanding of language, wisdom, learning, and how to combine the classical and the innovative.

Happily, all those collections are now available together in O'Siadhail's recently published *Collected Poems*.[1] Since the Gospel of John, my other main text, is part of the most widely available book in the world, I trust that, whatever readers may make of my understanding of them, they will be able to access these writings for themselves. I hope they might be stimulated to do the sort of reading and rereading of John and O'Siadhail that is recommended in chapter 4.

The third key element, interwoven with the Gospel of John and O'Siadhail's poetry, is life today. On this I have risked being more autobiographical than in *The Shape of Living*. The past fifteen years have mostly been a continuation of what chapter 1 calls the "ordinary drama" of my life with others in family, friendships, church, various communities and causes, teaching, research, administration, and so on. These are always in the background, but at several points they come to the fore, as in some influential figures in my early life, experiences of interviewing, the way the centrality of the face-to-face was brought home to me through particular teachers and thinkers over many years; friendship with Micheal O'Siadhail; marriage to Deborah; a L'Arche retreat; personal prayer practices; my mother's aging; the death of my father-in-law, Daniel Hardy; and the love of jazz. I have also been involved to some extent in a few more public dramas, such as the time in post-genocide Rwanda, the performance of Shakespeare in Broadmoor, and interfaith engagement around the world.

Why choose the Gospel of John? I have long been fascinated by it. It has perhaps been the single most influential Christian theological work, and it continues to be of great importance among and beyond the world's Christians. It is one of the most mysterious texts—scholars differ about who wrote it; when or in what stages it was written; where and for whom it was written; what were the main influences on it; how it was received in the early church; how it relates to the Synoptics (the other three Gospels), to the letters of John, and to the rest of the New Testament; how historically reliable it is; what its purpose is; and much else. The history of its interpretation is vast, complex, and conflictual, and controversies continue to surround it today. It is also a text that is heard, read, and reflected on by millions of people around the world and enters into worship, liturgies, sermons, hymns, music, art, sculpture, film, and many websites.

Some time ago, I spent five years working with Frances Young on Paul's second letter to the Corinthians. It was a memorable time, trying to fathom one short, extraordinarily intense text and think through its meaning and implications for today.[2] That good experience made the even more demanding task of interpreting John's Gospel more attractive, and this is what I am now immersed in—and contracted to write a commentary on it. Writing the present book in dialogue with John has been quite a change from commenting on one chapter after another. It has stimulated new thoughts and given felicitous surprises, illustrating what John himself knew well: the fruitfulness of intertextuality, bringing rich texts into conversation with each other. But above all, it has brought home to me how daring John is and how he wants his readers to be comparably daring. The repeated rereading of John's Gospel for the chapters of this book has confirmed from many angles the sense that, not only is it thoroughly dramatic, but it also daringly improvises on its own sources; in addition, it encourages further improvisation by readers as part of being led **into all the truth** (16:13)—what my subtitle calls "becoming wise in the Spirit."

Why choose the poetry of Micheal O'Siadhail? First, there is something about good poetry in general. I love the density and depth of meaning combined with stimulation to reimagine and rethink, and the ways in which forms, rhythms, and the play of language are inseparable from that meaning. It is language to be savored, lingered over, meditated on, slowly absorbed, indwelt. In O'Siadhail, there is all that and more. I am, of course, biased, but I do not know of a better living poet in English.

We have also been friends for more than forty years; I am "first reader" of his poetry, and he of my theology. This has been one of the most important elements of my life and thought, but somehow until now it has been rather muted and indirect in the published work.[3] Part of writing this book has been a sense of liberation, bringing together the poetry and the theology with something like the freedom of continual interplay and improvisation that are part of the friendship and our daily conversations by phone or Skype. This book has felt like a new genre, only partly realized in *The Shape of Living*. The character of O'Siadhail's poetry—wide ranging, both public and personal, bringing head, heart, and practical living together, and using both classical and new poetic forms—has been well suited to the themes of this book.

There has also been the possibility of reading and discussing together particular poems—chapter 7, for example, is the outcome of some wonderful hours in Dublin opening up "Only End." So through the writing of this book there has been the strange experience of living very differently with the two main conversation partners: able to talk with and meet Micheal O'Siadhail, while John has remained as mysterious as ever, his authorship and most other aspects of the Fourth Gospel diversely understood (is "he" even male? or just one person?) by the books piled high in my study—the authors are men and women, Christian and non-Christian, scholars and theologians, poets and novelists, music and art critics, preachers and prophets, saints and spiritual guides from across two millennia and all continents.

I return to what I consider the heart of this project: the desirability and wisdom of reading and rereading, alone and with others, this Gospel and this poetry. I believe that it is through such rereading, such savoring of deep, generative texts, that we are best prepared for life, both in its ordinary and public dramas. Within those dramas, it is a rehearsal for loving and for dying, but, more even than that, it is an actual performance of our relationship with God and an indwelling of meanings that help to shape us.

In a book with a stress on improvisation, it is natural to ask, what next? The DNA of Bible, contemporary poetry, and life today that came together in *The Shape of Living*, and is developed in this book, could, I hope, be taken still further. There is much more in the Bible (indeed, in John's Gospel) to be explored, and I would especially like to engage more with the Tanakh/Old Testament. O'Siadhail is still writing; indeed, among the projects he is working on at present is his largest single work yet, which he aims to finish by 2017. Both the personal and public dramas also continue, and likewise the search for wisdom. So there may be a third in the series, and even that might not be the end.

Finally, there are two practical notes. The first is about the pronunciation of Micheal O'Siadhail: it is *Mee-hawl O'Sheel*.

The second is about two features of the way the book is printed. Biblical quotations are in bold and without quotation marks (unless someone is being quoted)—e.g., **In the beginning . . .** (John 1:1). Poetry (and Jean Vanier's prose) is in italics and also without quotation marks—e.g., *In the beginning . . .* ("So," *Tongues*).

# The Drama of Living

*Public and Ordinary*

The Gospel of John is perhaps the most dramatic book of the New Testament. After an opening that sets its story within the horizon of God and all reality, all life, and all people, it moves into a series of well-crafted scenes. John the Baptist meets Jesus; the first disciples follow Jesus; a wedding is flooded with wine; vendors and money-changers are driven out of the temple in Jerusalem; Nicodemus comes to Jesus by night; a Samaritan woman has her life transformed when she meets Jesus at a well; there are healings, a feeding, arguments, teachings; and Lazarus is called out of his tomb. On the night before his death, Jesus takes the role of a slave and washes his disciples' feet, then talks intensively with them, above all about love, the gift of the Holy Spirit, and their relationship with each other, himself, and his Father. The plot climaxes with Jesus's arrest, trial, crucifixion,

1

and resurrection. Then at the very end of all this drama, in the last chapter of the Gospel, there are two forward-looking scenes. The first suggests public drama with well-known "names" and big events; the second has an unnamed central character and suggests the ordinary drama of everyday life. But love is at the heart of both.

## Public Drama and Us

### Peter the Knot-Tier

The first centers on Simon Peter. Earlier, after Jesus was arrested, Peter had three times denied knowing him. Now, he is asked three times by Jesus, **Do you love me?** and three times is told, **Feed my lambs/sheep** (John 21:15, 16, 17). Then his martyr's death is predicted. In the New Testament, Peter is very much a leading spokesman for the disciples and the public face of the young church; it is no accident that the popes still trace their authority back to him. His is a high-profile name in the drama of history. Micheal O'Siadhail in *Globe* gives several condensed biographies of such people, preceded by a description of their role in "Traces," a series of sonnets:

> Still there are a few marked out for greatness.
> Remember debates: history maketh the man
> Or the other way around so that some innateness
> Chooses doers and heroes catch as catch can.
> Surely both a meaning someone wagers on,
> A lifelong preparation, but also no doubt
> The way it happens, this or that liaison,
> The fall and ravel of how it all plays out,
> Every complex motive we sift and sieve,
> The strands given, lines we splice or tie,
> Node-workers, knot-tiers, hitch-makers.
> Slowly we become our own movers and shakers

2

> As plot and characters merge in reasons why,
> Our histories still the tangle of lives we live.[1]

Peter, too, combines a meaning that he wagered his life on with the apparent happenstance of being there when Jesus was around. He was both chosen and had to respond to his call—*strands given*, but also ropes he himself had to *splice or tie*. Through the Gospels and the Acts of the Apostles we see him slowly, sometimes through mistakes and bitter experience (most agonizingly when he denied that he knew Jesus), becoming one of the *movers and shakers* in the tangle of the early church's life. He leaps to key conclusions (most penetratingly **You are the Messiah**—Mark 8:29) and addresses the large crowd on the day of Pentecost when the disciples go public with the news of Jesus's death and resurrection. Above all, in one of the most important events in the history of Christianity since Pentecost, Peter is the key actor in the extension of the church from Jews to others. The story of this transformation of early Christian identity, involving dreams, the breaking of biblical rules, preaching, experiences of the Holy Spirit, baptisms, discussion, decision making, and ongoing vehement argument, is told in Acts 10–11 and Galatians 1–2. It is about Peter as *knot-tier* and *hitch-maker*, inaugurating a new period in Christian history by bringing together Jews and non-Jews into one community. It is no accident that "tying the knot" or "getting hitched" is used for marriage, an event that has long-term, transgenerational consequences.

### Dramas of Public Life, Making Appointments, and the Media

Much of our sense of history, of current affairs, and of the groups with which we identify, such as nations, religions, political parties, or sports teams, comes from following the actions of public figures. It is often their response to controversial

3

issues, crises, or "the big moment" that makes or breaks their reputations. But judging them fairly calls for assessing their record over years. In dramatic terms, it is looking at the plot of their career, how it shows their abilities, their character, and the quality of their contribution. What knots have they tied that have held fast? So those who vote for politicians, or who appoint judges, leaders of organizations, or any other holder of a post of responsibility, look carefully at their record and CV. They assess the previous acts and scenes in their lives, and ask for references nominated by themselves and others in order to find reliable testimony. Has there been *a lifelong preparation* for this role?

Then comes the vital judgment: What about the future? What are the indications that this person will do well in a particular role as future scenes and acts unfold? Will she serve us well as a member of parliament? Will he be a good headmaster? Will this officer lead well under fire? Will this manager cope with greater responsibility? Which cardinal is up to becoming Pope? Which of the people seeking this role will be the "mover and shaker" we need?

This is the point at which *plot and characters merge in reasons why*, and we must weigh those reasons and take the risk of improvising the ongoing drama. The parallel with drama in a theater or a "television soap" breaks down—they are usually scripted. Now, we are into unscripted time. It is necessary to make a decision with no certain outcome.

Over several decades, I have been involved in dozens of such decisions, often in the course of appointing people to academic or church positions, though also as a representative on various appointing committees, as a voter, and as a member of a trade union and other bodies. It has been a mixed record—some decisions were wonderfully vindicated, some had ambiguous results, some "obviously right" decisions proved badly wrong, and some appointees were trusted and betrayed the trust. I am especially fascinated by the elements that count most for different people in trying to imagine the future of a nation, a city, a school, a trade union, a professional society, a university, or a family. Without a ready-made script, we all have to improvise. But what feeds into our improvisations?

During the final stage of an appointment process, for example, there are usually many elements on the table—job description, personal description, CV, references, reports on informal meetings with the candidate, and opinions on the presentation that has been made and on the main interview. Yet all of these have to be interpreted, and they may contain contradictions among themselves. Beyond that, those making the decision may not agree, and beyond what is tabled there is vast room for further differences. Nowadays, human resources professionals sometimes try to reduce the room for disagreements (and later grievance complaints) by rigidly defining criteria and procedures. They are above all out to reduce risk and increase control. The result is that they try to script the process in advance, reducing the opportunity for improvisation, whether good or bad. You are simply not allowed by the rules to break away from the agreed list and ask the question that might reveal most about a particular candidate. The control exercised can work against recognizing the "drama of living," with all its particularities, risks, and contingencies. It also tends, for better or worse, to eliminate (or at least forbid making explicit) larger perspectives due to beliefs, worldviews, cultures, values, or long-term visions. It claims a sort of "objectivity" or "neutrality," which on closer examination often turns out to be deeply biased toward a particular set of debatable values, judgments, and ways of exercising power.

In political life, the democratic process is at its best intensely dramatic. This has always made it suspect to those who above all prize control and the elimination of risk. There are, of course, many ways to attempt to influence it, not least by spending large sums on access to media and employing professional persuaders. But in societies with some diversity of opinion and conviction in their public debates, there is virtually endless scope for interpreting the records of candidates and governments; for advocating particular worldviews, sets of values, and visions of the future; and above all for genuine argument and decision between alternatives. Democracy in practice has great problems (though many would agree with Winston Churchill that, while it may be a bad method of government, it is better than all the others that have been tried), but it matches well with an approach to human life that gives primacy to its dramatic character.

The media themselves testify to this primacy by giving such prominence to drama in many forms: real-life news stories, interviews, and documentaries; fictional films and "soaps"; competitive sports; and contests in everything from apprenticing, baking, cooking, dating, and dancing to "faking it," super-nannying, quizzes, and onstage amateur talent performances. Celebrities of the entertainment world who figure in fictional dramas, sports, or other carefully devised contests are frequently better known and more influential than "real" characters in the spheres of politics, war, business, law, education, health, development, or crime.

### The Characters Who Shape Us

So, as ordinary people carrying on with daily life, our memories and imaginations are crowded with the dramas of the famous. As we shape our lives and cope with new situations, the characters from history, fiction, and all those media dramas offer us scenarios and possibilities with which to imagine ourselves and our future. They are part of the material we use to think with and to make judgments and decisions. So it really matters which characters grip us most. To whom do we return again and again? Who is built into our consciousness as a model, example, saint, hero, or heroine? And who is the bad example, the antihero, or the character complex enough to stimulate constant rethinking? Over the years, most of us build up a cast of characters beyond the people we know personally. We live with them and identify with their dramas. They people our days and often our night dreams. They are intrinsic to the meaning we find in life—they embody what means most to us. Like friends, there is not room for very many in one life.

It is worth asking ourselves who these key figures in our lives are. Some play a vital role for a while—not so much a walk-on part as a leading character in one scene. Others are woven into our lives over many years, accompanying decade after decade. Among the long-term characters in my own life to whom I have been drawn, beyond those in the Bible, include Dietrich Bonhoeffer, whose life, death, and writings first took hold of me as a teenager and continue to be generative. Some other "early loves" from student days have stood the test of time. Alexander Solzhenitsyn's novels and accounts of the labor camps of the Soviet Union's Gulag Archipelago opened up a world of suffering, good, and evil that has continued to be a key reference point. J. S. Bach, especially his B Minor Mass; Cézanne's still lifes and landscapes; Rembrandt's faces; Patrick Kavanagh in his poem "Lough Derg" and the remarkable body of poems he wrote after coming out of the hospital in middle age; George Herbert, through his poetry and collection of proverbs; the Greek historian Thucydides and his contemporary Sophocles the tragedian; Socrates and Plato; Henri Le Saux (Abhishiktananda), a French Dominican monk who spent decades in India and whose little book on prayer was a breakthrough in learning to pray; Simone Weil; Shakespeare;

C. S. Lewis, who first made an impact on me through his accounts of what Christianity is, later through reading his Chronicles of Narnia to my children, and most recently through his complex, probing, late novel *Till We Have Faces*; St. Thérèse of Lisieux through her autobiography; and George Eliot, mainly through *Middlemarch*. Others have entered later in life, but reviewing them now, it is striking how durable and fruitful these early influences have been, worth returning to again and again.

O'Siadhail in *Globe* writes a series of biographical poems about some of his key figures and the history-making "knots" they tied—his epigraph for this section is from Chaucer: "The knotte, that why every tale is toold. . . ." They are Gregor Mendel, botanist; Emmanuel Levinas, philosopher; Patrick Kavanagh, poet; Shakespeare; Jean Vanier, founder of the L'Arche communities for those with and without learning disabilities; Sigrid Undset, Norwegian novelist; Nelson Mandela; Gandhi of India; Bartolomé de las Casas, defender of native rights in Latin America; and Máirtín Ó Cadhain, Irish novelist.

Each of us will have our own list—it is worth reflecting on it, and whether anyone else should join it. One of the great delights of life is to share a key figure with a friend.

For Jews, Christians, Muslims, and many others, the Bible has been a rich source for such characters. Just in the Gospel of John, there are those from the Tanakh/Old Testament such as Abraham, Moses, and Isaiah, whom John also shares with the Qur'an; some he shares with the other Gospels such as John the Baptist, Peter, the mother of Jesus and Joseph, Judas, Pontius Pilate, Joseph of Arimathea, and Mary Magdalene; others he alone has, such as Nicodemus and the Samaritan woman at the well. John is rewriting the tradition—for example, by pairing Peter with the beloved disciple. To meditate on the Gospel of John is to find that the up-front role of Peter leads time and again into noticing how this other unnamed character is even more important, and that both of them draw us deeper into the God-centered drama that is still ongoing.

## The Dramas That Shape Us

O'Siadhail follows his poems on individual characters with another series on historical tragedies: the wiping out of most Bushmen in the Kalahari Desert; the killing of most Eastern European Jews in the Nazi Holocaust; the continuing Palestinian conflict; slavery in the United States; the Armenian genocide; the wiping out of Hiroshima by the first atomic bomb; the "blotting out" of the Ainu in Japan; Cromwell's massacres in Ireland; and English suppression of the Irish language and culture. As we read them, and also follow the news, we can see such things still happening. We are part of the human history in which these and similar things occur. It is a distinct shock to think that I was alive not only during the Rwandan genocide but also during the Cambodian "killing fields" of Pol Pot, the Bosnian ethnic cleansing, the Chinese Cultural Revolution, and the massacres in Darfur.

But what on earth should we do about it? Are we as impotent as we usually feel? Considering such events of horror, terror, hatred, cruelty, malice, coldheartedness, organized violence, and evil, it would be easy to despair or to become resigned, hardened, cynical. O'Siadhail wrestles with this too. "Crying Out," the powerful culminating poem of the series, reflects on all these tragedies. Two lessons stand out.

First, we need to *face and word* the truth, to remember, and to practice *patient listening*:

> The long mute pleas of the dead
> For us to remember things
> So beyond our ken we barely control

9

Our deepest urge to shun in dread
Their clammy-handed nobblings,
To flee the ghostly buttonhole

Of those whose testimony shocks
Too much for us to hear.
Of patterns we're destined to rehearse

Unless a patient listening unblocks
Such clogged up fear
Of our histories' ancient mariners,

Voyages we need to face and word,
Stories of dreams still-born,
Tragedies that never found a voice,

Cries of agony yet to be heard.
So much we must mourn
Until our broken bones rejoice. [2]

There, Coleridge's *Rime of the Ancient Mariner*, a classic poem
of remembered trauma, provides the image of insistent testimony to what is most difficult to take in. O'Siadhail understands
that silence, avoidance, and failure to learn lessons run the terrible risk of increasing the danger that history will be repeated:

But out of our darkest silences now instead
We risk becoming everything we dread:

The fractured clamour of each remembering victim
As deaf to the world as the world was once to them.

With too many memories and our psyche smothers.
Will our victimhood learn to keep this word for others?

This lesson culminates with a passionate appeal:

Memory, mother of muses,
wake us, shake us up out of this haunted
past that will not pass.

Second, we would be advised to follow O'Siadhail by entering more deeply into a select few of these tragedies. Just as we can take to heart a few well-known people, and they can become the ones we look to, as we identify with them and live our lives in their light, so we can choose especially to remember certain events—O'Siadhail even compares it to making friends:

> As we choose a friend
> In the end
> We blend or select memories to mend
> Whatever engine moves
> Our spirits on,
>
> But don't efface
> The place
> Or trace of any lost or wounded face
> Stained with its loves and lives
> From our horizon.

One of my daughters, Rebecca, did fieldwork for her social anthropology dissertation in a genocide survivors' community in Rwanda, where nearly one million people were killed within a hundred days in 1994. The community invited her and our whole family back for Christmas, so the five of us went there in December 2009. We were immersed in the aftermath of the genocide. We had intensive conversations with survivors and with several who had studied it and thought about it. We learned how survivors were being helped, we visited genocide sites and a well-designed museum, and we read testimonies and histories. One of the most moving memorials was a room full of photographs of children killed, traces of each *lost . . . face*, with short biographies. We were all overwhelmed and are still trying to come to terms with it. It has left us with something unforgettable, something to return to repeatedly, with many questions. It relativizes many of our concerns and priorities.

It also raises acutely the problem of meaning. What sense can be made of such an event? Is not learning more about it (and about other events such as O'Siadhail responds to) a recipe for despair and meaninglessness? For some it has been so, and tragedy—or even something more like the theater of the absurd—has been for them the last word, sometimes leading to suicide. But it is also striking how for others it has been the opposite. They have somehow come to a deeper meaning.

The community in Kigali where we were living was Christian. Rwanda itself was over 90 percent Christian at the time of the 1994 genocide. Christians killed other Christians in huge numbers. It was common for members of the same church congregation to include both hunters and hunted as the Tutsi fled from the Hutu into forests and marshes. Yet despite the horror of killing, torture, and humiliation being compounded by most of its perpetrators being fellow Christians, many of those we met were finding in their faith the resources for new life. There was agonized questioning and no sense at all of forgetting the horrors—on the contrary, there was both group and individual counseling that included retelling the stories of what these survivors had been through. But at the same time there was a sense that meaning could be found by going deeper into the gospel, taking the crucified and risen Jesus even more seriously. The disciples Jesus himself had chosen included Peter who denied him and Judas who betrayed him to the enemies who killed him. More fundamentally, Jesus is the One who has been through death.

There was a stunning demonstration of what this meant at a worship service on the Sunday after Christmas, for which about seven hundred members of genocide-survivors communities from across Rwanda gathered. They included a large group of widows who sat together—most of those present were widows or orphans. At one point in the five-hour service a troupe of young people entered, energetically dancing to the beat of drums.

Some of the dancers were old enough to have been through the genocide, others had been born after it—so they represented both the children the widows had lost and the children they had not been able to have, either because their husbands had been killed or because they themselves had been so badly tortured and raped (and often infected with HIV/AIDS) that they could no longer bear children. When the dancers appeared, suddenly a wave of uncontrollable weeping swept through the widows. The weeping and the dancing continued together, grief and joy. It seemed like a demonstration of the double realism of the faith of the community: the realism of the cross, with the continuing fact of suffering, grief, and irreparable loss; and the realism of the resurrection, affirming life, community, hope, and joy, and not letting suffering, death, and evil have the last word:

> So much we must mourn
> Until our broken bones rejoice.

Traumatic, genocidal dramas are extreme, but, like death itself (see chapter 6), it is wise to take them to heart. To ignore them is to risk escapism, lack of proportion, and insensitivity to a world where such things happen, quite apart from the danger that even more might happen if we fail to remember and ponder them. Yet there are many other public dramas to engage with in all spheres of society, and through films, novels, plays, and soaps. Some have their own extremes and extraordinary aspects, from war and crime to vampires and magic, but many hold a mirror up to ordinary lives and situations. The last chapter of the Gospel of John sets up this mirror, too.

*Ordinary Drama: The Unnamed Disciple,*
*the Unnamed Mother, and Us*

John 21 begins with some of the disciples of Jesus, on Peter's initiative, returning to their previous occupation of fishing. Jesus

13

appears on the beach and directs them so that they take a large catch, but he is not recognized until **that disciple whom Jesus loved said to Peter, "It is the Lord!"** (v. 7). Jesus cooks breakfast of fish and bread for them on a charcoal fire and then has the conversation with Peter in which Peter affirms his love for Jesus three times and is told three times to feed Jesus's lambs and sheep. So Peter is directed to the daily, repetitive, essential task of sustaining and nourishing the community of those who follow Jesus. His public life as a leader; his testing in which **when you grow old, you will stretch out your hands, and someone else will fasten a belt around you and take you where you do not wish to go**; and the predicted **death by which he would glorify God** (John 21:18–19) are all in the service of loving Jesus and serving his community year after year till he is old and then is executed.

Immediately after this exchange with Jesus **Peter turned and saw the disciple whom Jesus loved following them; he was the one who had reclined next to Jesus** [literally, lay on Jesus's breast] **at the supper and had said, "Lord, who is it that is going to betray you?" When Peter saw him, he said to Jesus, "Lord, what about him?" Jesus said to him, "If it is my will that he remain until I come, what is that to you? Follow me!"** (John 21:20–22). The mysterious, much-discussed character, **the disciple whom Jesus loved**, makes at least four appearances at key points in the story, but is perhaps assumed to be present throughout (see John 21:24). As this quotation reminds us, he was there, closest to Jesus at the Last Supper before his betrayal (13:23); he also stood with Jesus's mother at the cross as Jesus died; he was at the empty tomb on Easter morning and was the first to believe in the resurrection of Jesus. He is unnamed, and one way of taking that is that he stands for any of us.

Peter is the named leader, the public face of the church who dies for his Lord; the beloved disciple stands for those to whom Jesus means a great deal and who lead a far more ordinary life.

Interestingly, John often pairs the two. This may even happen at the very beginning of the Gospel when Peter is given his new name by Jesus. Just before this, one of the first two disciples to follow Jesus is unnamed, and many scholars think this is the beloved disciple (John 1:35–42). The beloved disciple is explicitly said to be present with Peter at the Last Supper, at the empty tomb, and now with the risen Jesus but not, of course, at the crucifixion of Jesus, because Peter had denied and deserted him.

For the beloved disciple, on the contrary, the crucifixion is the setting for the one event to which he is central: **When Jesus saw his mother and the disciple whom he loved standing beside her, he said to his mother, "Woman, here is your son." Then he said to the disciple, "Here is your mother." And from that hour the disciple took her into his own home** (John 19:26–27). This is about home life, the heart of ordinariness. Two of the people closest to Jesus, his mother and the disciple repeatedly called "beloved," are brought by him into a new, family-like relationship and form a household together.

This connects with the only other appearance of the mother of Jesus in John's Gospel (where she is never named—perhaps she too is someone with whom everyone is invited to identify). Jesus gives the first "sign" of who he is, his first meaning-laden act, not in public (that follows immediately afterward, in the Jerusalem temple), but at a wedding, a private affair (John 2:1–12). In this story, he responds to an appeal from his mother about an embarrassing domestic crisis, the fact that the wine has run out, by turning a huge amount of water into very good wine. In the context of the Tanakh/Old Testament and the Synoptic Gospels (those of Matthew, Mark, and Luke), that John should choose to lead with this scene is distinctive and full of symbolism about marriage, water, wine, abundance, and the significance of Jesus. But for our present purposes two things are especially worth noting. One is the precedence given to this domestic event over the following one in the temple—Jesus is first of all involved in the celebration of something that happens in all cultures, an event in the life cycle that represents the continuation of family life and the importance of love, promises, home, sex, children, property, and much else.

The other is the sharp exchange with his mother. When she says that the wine has run out he responds: **"Woman, what concern is that to you and to me? My hour has not yet come"** (John 2:4). Scholars debate just what the Greek means, but it seems clear that at the least this is a distancing statement. Jesus calls her **"woman"** rather than "mother," just as he does from the cross. This lacks intimacy and together with the fact that she is not named may also invite us to see her as a representative woman. **My hour**, which in John refers to his coming death, then introduces Jesus's particular calling, why he is sent by God, pointing forward (most clearly for those rereading the Gospel—see chapter 4 below on rereading) to the second appearance of his mother at his crucifixion. So there is a distancing from his natural family in the interests of his calling on behalf of other people.

It is also striking that there is no rejection of his mother in favor of his disciples. On the contrary, this wedding feast brings together Jesus's recently called disciples with his mother, and then **after this he went down to Capernaum with his mother, his brothers, and his disciples; and they remained there a few days** (John 2:12). So the emphasis here is on Jesus being with both his family and his disciples. John even uses one of his favorite multileveled words to describe them being together: the Greek verb *menein*, here translated **remained**, can also mean "abide," "stay," "continue," "rest." Already by this stage in his Gospel, John has used it of the Holy Spirit resting on Jesus (twice, 1:32–33) and of the first disciples staying with him (twice, 1:38–39). Later, its use will climax in the parable of the vine, ten times in ten verses (15:1–10), as Jesus speaks of the daily ongoing life of faith: **Those who abide in me and I in them bear much fruit. . . . As the Father has loved me, so I have loved you; abide in my love** (15:5, 9). The last use is in the final chapter about the beloved disciple: "**If it is my will that he remain until I come . . .**" (twice, 21:22–23). That "remaining" is in his home with the mother of Jesus. It is a new, family-like community that includes, but is not limited to, the natural family and is headlined at the beginning of the Gospel (1:12–13).

Two fundamental elements of such ordinary living are the relative obscurity of what goes on in it—its lack of public visibility—and its dependence on being sustained by promises, commitments, habits, disciplines, and routines. The first is emphasized in the last of the five sonnets of O'Siadhail's "Traces"; the second runs through many poems in O'Siadhail's *Love Life*.

*Stories No One Has Told*

If extreme events such as genocides raise radical questions of meaning, others arise from the ordinariness of life that has *nothing momentous*:

> For most nothing momentous or too high-flown,
> Just some trace laid down, our mark made
> In the give and take of lives, a loan of a loan
> Passed on as mention of our names will fade.
> It's mainly fallen angels with our clayed feet
> And yet moments in stories no one has told,
> Split seconds of our double time, a pleat
> In a cloth of histories that takes so long to unfold.
> A promise kept, something done for someone
> As rumours of decency gone to ground for years
> Re-emerge, the way suddenly in a niece's son
> A gene that ducked and weaved then reappears;
> Gestures of love on streets of a fragile city,
> Memory inscribed in action, a scratch on eternity.[3]

The last couplet's mention of *love* and *eternity* hint at a God's-eye view of dailyness: it really matters how we make our mark *in the give and take of lives*. The little "knots" of decency and love may be just as significant in God's sight as the *momentous* knots of history that are tied by Peter or presidents or generals—and even these are in most of their lives mainly occupied with apparently smaller matters. For most of us, *our names will fade*; but we are responsible for *traces* that can be as long lasting as genes, scratches inscribed on eternity in the language of love. Our ordinary face-to-face encounters (as explored in chapter 3) are a primary location of the meaning of life.

The last scene in John's Gospel, after twice reminding us of the "remaining/abiding" of the beloved disciple, then gives the final words of Jesus to Peter: "**Follow me!**" (21:22; cf. 21:19). In the light of the rest of the Gospel, this is a call to continue with the drama of loving.

*Habits of Love*

That drama is not just about events and moments of *double time*: it is crucially also a matter of habits, patterns, and regularities repeated year after year and sustained by faithfulness and commitments. O'Siadhail's *Love Life* covers several decades of his marriage and frequently dwells on such formative continuities over time. In "Echo-sounder," he describes the marriage by drawing on images of a monk's days shaped by liturgy, a pianist's hands that have mastered a melody, an expert writer of Chinese characters, and the skills of handling a sailing boat. These are all practices that require learning, discipline, dedication, and time.

> A life's canonical rhythm,
> Monk-like tempo of days;
> Muscle, sinew, limb
> Learn mundane strategies,

Passages crossed, re-crossed,
Courses steered by degrees
As a pianist's fingered trust
Sleeps across the keys,

Or wrist movements retain
Ordered strokes of Chinese
Characters, a graven routine
Which both ties and frees.

Hoists and binds that gird
Days of rites and liturgies,
Halyard and curtain cord
Clothes lines, hanked stays.

Echoes in a mind's chamber
As a boat heels and sways
Stirs a cradle we remember
To lull a freshening breeze.

A wind-moment's once-off
And ready-about novices
We wear our habits of love.
Even keel of our ease.[4]

A good day's sailing, a letter in Chinese, a well-played piano
concerto, a moving liturgy: these do not happen without hours
and years of attentive practice, and the making of many mistakes—and neither does a good marriage, a peaceful community, or a fruitful life. John's abiding/remaining/continuing is
the secret of fruitfulness, shaped by our habits of mind, heart,
and body. The "echo-sounder" of the poem's title is the sailor's
device for finding out how deep the water is. Here, the echoes
are *in a mind's chamber*, going down to the primal memory of
being rocked in a cradle, as in a boat. John too, as later chapters
will explore, sounds the depths of primal memories through
symbols such as language, light and darkness, water, food and

drink, abiding in love, and being called by name—all, as it happens, experienced first when we are in the cradle. The lines

> Stirs a cradle we remember
> To lull a freshening breeze

defy paraphrase, arouse memories, and evoke many levels, as do the deep Johannine symbols. For now, they are an apt opening into the final section of this chapter: the sense of abiding at the heart of family life, in communion with those who love us, combines with a wind that can blow unpredictably, but the *lull* ensures that in the face of an uncertain future, it is peace and the *habits of love*, not the anxieties of insecurity, that clothe us.

### The Drama of Living with Jesus: Ongoing Improvisation in the Spirit

In the last chapter of John, we have focused mostly on Peter and the beloved disciple, but the main character is Jesus. Jesus asks Peter: **"Do you love me?"** The future-oriented point of the chapter is the repeated **"Follow me!"** The double invitation is to love and be loved by Jesus and to play a part in his continuing drama. The whole of the Gospel of John is written to enable this loving, being loved, and following.

At the heart of John's approach are the two distinctive new elements of Christianity: the coming of Jesus and the giving of the Holy Spirit. They are, of course, there in the other Gospels too, but John intensifies, simplifies, and deepens the concentration on them. In a remarkable development, he both crafts the drama of Jesus's life, death, and resurrection around the question of who Jesus is and he also encourages daring Spirit-led improvisation in the ongoing drama.

Who is Jesus? John's Gospel has perhaps been the single most influential book in the history of Christian theology, especially in Christology, the doctrine of the person of Jesus Christ. John's Prologue (1:1–18) alone has been one of the most discussed texts century after century. For now, the key point is that, for all the importance of the Prologue, the main way John tells us who Jesus is, is through the rest of the Gospel, and this is in the form of one dramatic encounter with Jesus after another.

It is carefully written to answer the question, who is Jesus? in multiple ways and at many levels, so the reader is constantly led to reread; to make new connections with the rest of the Gospel, the Synoptics, and the Tanakh/Old Testament; and to explore what the meaning might be of capacious, symbolic statements such as **"I am the bread of life"** (6:35), **"I am the light of the world"** (8:12), **"I am the way, and the truth, and the life"** (14:6), and many others. Such open, dense descriptions cry out to be meditated on again and again, and no one ever comes to the end of this process. The theological reason for this is simple: Jesus, who is identified through this drama and these statements, is alive and is present as God is present, so the Gospel is actually a means of relating to him in person, and no one ever comes to the end of that. One of John's favorite phrases, "eternal life," is not so much about "life after death" as "life after the death and resurrection of Jesus"—life, with others, abiding in him, loved by him, and loving him (this approach to love and to death will be explored further in chapters 5 and 6). It is, as the title of O'Siadhail's book says, *Love Life*.

The way Jesus is portrayed in the Gospel story is the main inspiration for our ideas and images of who Jesus is. It both disciplines our tendency to fantasize and to create self-serving or distorted images, and it frees us to go deeper and further, using our minds and imaginations in prayer, conversation, theology, the arts, relating to creation and other people, and acting in the

21

world. In other words, it is central in shaping our participation in the ongoing drama initiated by "**Follow me!**"

John of all the Gospels is most concerned with the transition to the time when Jesus is no longer physically present with his followers. Much of the Farewell Discourse in John 13–17 is about preparing the disciples for this time. In an astonishing promise Jesus says, "**Very truly, I tell you, the one who believes in me will also do the works that I do and, in fact, will do greater works than these, because I am going to the Father. I will do whatever you ask in my name, so that the Father may be glorified in the Son**" (John 14:12–13). Besides this, there is also a promise that "**when the Spirit of truth comes, he will guide you into all the truth**" (John 16:13–14). The secret of doing **greater works** and being led **into all the truth** is the gift of the Holy Spirit, also called the Spirit of truth and the *paraklētos*, a Greek word meaning "advocate," "encourager," "strengthener," "comforter," "helper"—literally "one who stands alongside and cries out or calls out or is called upon."

The vital point is that the Spirit both looks back to remind disciples of Jesus and inspires them in what they say and do in the continuing drama. So, on the one hand, "**The Advocate, the Holy Spirit, whom the Father will send in my name, will teach you everything, and remind you of all that I have said to you**" (14:26). On the other hand, when the resurrected Jesus fulfills his promise and breathes the Holy Spirit into his disciples, he says: "**Peace be with you. As the Father has sent me, so I send you**" (20:21). The reminding, the *echo-sounder* of remembering Jesus, and the sending of the *freshening breeze* of the Spirit, blowing into uncharted waters, are accompanied by the peace of the crucified and risen Jesus. Together, these enable the new improvisations—in thought, imagination, prayer, witness, action, and habit—that carry forward the drama of following Jesus in faith and love.

John wrote his Gospel as one who had received the Spirit and those promises. So it can be read as an example of what it means to remember Jesus and his teaching and to be guided into all the truth. His daring theology (which is being explored throughout this book) is **written so that you may come to believe that Jesus is the Messiah, the Son of God, and that through believing you may have life in his name** (20:31). It is a theology of abundant truth and life that recognizes that there is far more truth, light, and understanding than it contains. John gives a script that is not only to be repeated but is also to be improvised on. By calling others to believe in Jesus and to receive the Holy Spirit, John is inviting them to be led further into the truth and to do yet greater things. His own Gospel has been one of the most effective enablers of that, but in a world that is understood as coming into being through Jesus Christ, there are also many others. The next chapter follows through on the theme of wisdom and its improvisations in Scriptures, O'Siadhail, and others.

2

# Improvising Wisdom

*Within and between Traditions*

The pursuit of wisdom is found in most civilizations and their religious, philosophical, and cultural traditions. Even when the word "wisdom" is not used, it is often present through concerns for sound, intelligent judgment and decision making, prudent discernment of priorities, long-term flourishing of people and societies, the avoidance of foolishness and stupidity, and the combining of knowledge, values, and appropriate practices. Most of us would agree that wisdom is to be desired in a parent, a leader, a counselor, a teacher, and indeed in any responsible role and in everyone's life. At its best, it not only seeks overall meaning, understanding, and truth, both broad and deep, but also tries to connect this with practical responses to specific situations. Because both understanding and situations change, wisdom needs to improvise continually.

In this chapter, I begin in Alexandria in Egypt, a cradle of wisdom in several traditions, savor Micheal O'Siadhail's bringing together of a number of wisdom strands in his poem "Study," and then examine both the seeking of wisdom between religious traditions, as found in Scriptural Reasoning, and the wisdom of my own Christian tradition, as seen in the Gospel of John.

## Improvising Wisdom in Alexandria

Wisdom is radiant and unfading, and she is easily discerned by those who love her, and is found by those who seek her. She hastens to make herself known to those who desire her. One who rises early to seek her will have no difficulty, for she will be found sitting at the gate. To fix one's thought on her is perfect understanding, and one who is vigilant on her account will soon be free from care, because she goes about seeking those worthy of her, and she graciously appears to them in their paths, and meets them in every thought. The beginning of wisdom is the most sincere desire for instruction, and concern for instruction is love of her. . . .

I called on God, and the spirit of wisdom came to me. I preferred her to scepters and thrones, and I accounted wealth as nothing in comparison with her. Neither did I liken to her any priceless gem, because all gold is but a little sand in her sight, and silver will be accounted as clay before her. I loved her more than health and beauty, and I chose to have her rather than light, because her radiance never ceases. . . .

I learned without guile and I impart without grudging; I do not hide her wealth, for it is an unfailing treasure for mortals; those who get it obtain friendship with God, commended for the gifts that come from instruction. May God grant me to speak with judgment, and to have thoughts worthy of what I have received; for he is the guide even of wisdom and the corrector of the wise. For both we and our words are in his hand, as are all understanding and skill in crafts. For it is he who gave me unerring knowledge of what exists, to know the structure of the world and the activity of the elements; the beginning and end and middle of times, the alternations of the solstices and the changes of the seasons, the cycles of the year and the constellations of the stars, the natures of animals and the tempers of wild animals, the powers of spirits and the thoughts of human beings, the varieties of plants and the virtues of roots; I learned both what is secret and what is manifest, for wisdom, the fashioner of all things, taught me.

There is in her a spirit that is intelligent, holy, unique, manifold, subtle, mobile, clear, unpolluted, distinct, invulnerable, loving the good, keen, irresistible, beneficent, humane, steadfast, sure, free from anxiety, all-powerful, overseeing all, and penetrating through all spirits that are intelligent, pure, and altogether subtle. For wisdom is more mobile than any motion; because of her pureness she pervades and penetrates all things. For she is a breath of the power of God, and a pure emanation of the glory of the Almighty; therefore nothing defiled gains entrance into her. For she is a reflection of eternal light, a spotless mirror of the working of God, and an image of his goodness. Although she is but one, she can do all things, and while remaining in herself, she renews all things; in every generation she passes into holy souls and makes them friends of God, and prophets; for God loves nothing so much as the person who lives with wisdom. She is more beautiful than the sun, and excels every constellation of the stars. Compared with the light she is found to be superior, for it is succeeded by the night, but against wisdom evil does not prevail. . . .

I loved her and sought her from my youth; I desired to take her for my bride, and became enamored of her beauty. . . .

And if anyone loves righteousness, her labors are virtues; for she teaches self-control and prudence, justice and courage; nothing in life is more profitable for mortals than these. And if anyone longs for wide experience, she knows the things of old, and infers the things to come; she understands turns of speech and the solutions of riddles; she has foreknowledge of signs and wonders and of the outcome of seasons and times. Therefore I determined to take her to live with me, knowing that she would give me good counsel and encouragement in cares and grief. Because of her I shall have glory among the multitudes and honor in the presence of the elders, though I am young. I shall be found keen in judgment, and in the sight of rulers I shall be admired. . . .

When I enter my house, I shall find rest with her; for companionship with her has no bitterness, and life with her has no pain, but gladness and joy. When I considered these things inwardly, and pondered in my heart that in kinship with wisdom there is immortality, and in friendship with her, pure delight, and in the labors of her hands, unfailing wealth, and in the experience of her company, understanding, and renown in sharing her words, I went about seeking how to get her for myself. (Wisdom of Solomon 6–8)

That passionate praise of wisdom and learning was written over two millennia ago, probably by a Greek-speaking Jew in Alexandria, Egypt, who stood in a tradition of wisdom writing that was already then over a millennium old. The anonymous author lived in one of the greatest centers of learning and education of his world, and he is rethinking his (or her—the scholarly consensus is for a male author, but this may not be so) own tradition in engagement with others. There are signs of sharp tensions, and we know of anti-Jewish violence in Alexandria that may be part of the background of his polemics against Egyptian religion. In the midst of difficult, uncertain circumstances he goes deeper into his tradition and renews it for his time. Jewish wisdom had over the centuries been tested through many difficult times and had drawn on other ancient Near Eastern wisdom streams. The Bible had been written and edited with the help of their input.

The culminating achievement of Greek-speaking Judaism in Alexandria was the Septuagint, the translation of the Hebrew Scriptures into Greek. Septuagint means "seventy" (it is often referred to by the Roman numeral LXX), so called because of a story that seventy translators had each independently come up with the same translation. It is the sort of legend that both shows how important the Septuagint was and also that there was a need for reassurance about its authority—many felt uneasy about the inevitable changes of meaning that happen in translation, the distancing from the original Hebrew, and the danger of assimilation to pagan society through using its language. The question of translating Scriptures and other classic texts has provoked intense anxiety and conflict in many religions—in Western Christianity people such as John Wycliffe died in the cause of translating the Bible into the vernacular. We will return to this question in chapter 4 below, arguing that the risks of translations are more than compensated by the generativity of the rereadings they inspire.

The author of the Wisdom of Solomon wrote in Greek in the aftermath of the Hebrew Scriptures being translated. The Wisdom literature, such as Proverbs and Job, was side by side with what were considered the most authoritative books, the first five (Genesis, Exodus, Leviticus, Numbers, and Deuteronomy), called the Torah—inadequately rendered "law," *nomos* in Greek, but in fact having a broader sense of a "way of life." The Wisdom of Solomon undertakes to integrate the wisdom tradition with the Torah, especially the exodus from Egypt, so facing one of the perennial issues of Judaism and later of Christianity and Islam: how to combine and think together both the highly particular narratives, which give them their specific historical identity, and the traditions of learning, knowledge, and wisdom that resonate broadly with other cultures, civilizations, and religions and connect with their philosophies, languages, histories, arts, and sciences. Egypt was one of the main places where these issues were thought and argued about by pagans, Jews, Christians, and Muslims in the millennium after the Wisdom of Solomon was

written. And it is worth remembering that across the Middle
East, and in India, China, Tibet, Japan, Greece, and elsewhere,
other sophisticated wisdom traditions were at the same time
being passed on and developed.

The Wisdom of Solomon unites the passions for wisdom, for
continuing the drama of Israel's history, and for God. In the
passage quoted above, the passions for wisdom and God are
inseparable. **I called on God, and the spirit of wisdom came to
me.** When she comes, personified wisdom shapes the whole of
a person's life, from rising early in the morning to seek her and
finding her already waiting, to returning home to **rest with her**
at night. She is met with **in every thought** and is more highly
valued than power, wealth, health, and beauty. She is **intelligent,**
stretching minds to understand human life and history as well
as where it is heading—animals, plants, and **all things.** At the
same time, she is **holy . . . loving the good . . . beneficent, humane, steadfast . . . a spotless mirror of the working of God,
and an image of his goodness.** So intelligence is combined with
goodness and the virtues—**self-control and prudence, justice
and courage.** The classical Greek "transcendentals" of truth,
goodness, and beauty are completed by **her radiance . . . more
beautiful than the sun.** The practicalities of **skill in crafts . . .
good counsel and encouragement in cares and grief** and how
to relate to the powerful are also embraced by this capacious
reality of wisdom.

There is no sense here that anyone can ever master wisdom
or have a neat package of knowledge or faith in God. This God
of wisdom, goodness, and beauty is extraordinarily dynamic:
**manifold, subtle, mobile . . . all-powerful, overseeing all, and
penetrating through all spirits . . . For wisdom is more mobile
than any motion; because of her pureness she pervades and
penetrates all things. For she is a breath of the power of God,
and a pure emanation of the glory of the Almighty . . . she**

can do all things . . . against wisdom evil does not prevail. Life is therefore about sustaining alertness to the all-pervasive dynamic presence of God and God's wisdom, desiring, searching, and being open to new understanding and teaching. She is found by those who seek her. . . . The beginning of wisdom is the most sincere desire for instruction, and concern for instruction is love of her. . . . It is a life of continual learning and sharing what is learned: I learned without guile and I impart without grudging.

This is the spirit in which the author goes about improvising on Israel's drama. There can be no simple repetition of the past. For him, the wise way of being Jewish in the cosmopolitan, educated Hellenistic civilization of Alexandria is to be as intelligently faithful as possible, staying deeply rooted in the tradition while being open to fresh understanding and to constant rethinking and renewal: while remaining in herself, she renews all things. This is improvising wisdom at the heart of the dynamism of the drama of living.

## The Love of Wisdom and the Wisdom of Love

Yet I have passed over the most obvious feature of this praise of wisdom: the passion of being in love, desiring the beloved, and being loved. The life of wisdom is for those who love her . . . those who desire her. It is a love that is mutual, with the combined intensities and joys of friendship, marriage, and family: in every generation she passes into holy souls and makes them friends of God, and prophets; for God loves nothing so much as the person who lives with wisdom. . . . I loved her and sought her from my youth; I desired to take her for my bride, and became enamored of her beauty . . . in kinship with wisdom there is immortality, and in friendship with her, pure delight.

It is no accident that the author writes in the person of Solomon. He is the archetypal figure of wisdom in Israel's history, and the books of Proverbs and Ecclesiastes were traditionally ascribed to him too. But he was also the great lover, with many, many wives and concubines. The great love poem of the Bible, the Song of Songs, is also called the Song of Solomon. In her superb commentary on Proverbs, Ecclesiastes, and the Song of Songs, Ellen Davis makes a strong case for taking the three together.[1] They can be seen playing complementary roles in the education and formation of young men in Israel. So the love of wisdom and the wisdom of love accompany and illuminate each other.

Micheal O'Siadhail, in "Study,"[2] densely interweaves the themes of learning, understanding, insight, and tradition with those of love, family (mother, child, father), and marriage. It is one of a series of poems in *Love Life* in which he meditates on his home and the life that goes on there:

> Lovemaking, meals, guests, moments of despair,
> For all our secrets here these walls have ears.
> ("Trimleston," 496)

At the top of the house is the study:

> 1
>
> Here in our attic room
> I bend lovingly over my only heirloom,
> My mother's polished bureau,
>
> Drawing Japanese characters
> For the word study. Over and over I rehearse
> Twenty-one strokes,
>
> A half-stroke for each century
> Back to the Yellow River 2000 B.C.
> On bones and tortoise shells.

Strive and strong combine
To mean study. For study the first sign
A squatting figure, a woman's

Genitals and legs spread wide
Suggests birth struggle alongside
Tensed biceps for effort.

My strength a drawn bow,
I crouch in over my mother's bureau.
Love's hard labour.


2

Slow summers I recall
Reading for an autumn exam:
Lovely months of process.
No need for grind or cram,
Relishing each small
Detail, every finesse,
Crescendo of long haul.

Pulse and surge of insight,
Some falling into place,
Skull-thrill of illumination,
Glimpses in medias res,
Moments taking flight,
A child born again
In the aha! of delight.

Days when ideas churn
And settle, connections made,
A synapse tenses and eases,
Things grasped in delayed
Reaction, a dawning pattern
Distends my mind and pleases;
I think I'm happiest when I learn.

3

High in my dormer I see you hunching below
To nurture a patch slowly made your own,
Host to cuttings or shoots and happy although
The garden you work is always a loan of a loan.
Travail of signs borrowed from hand to hand,
As I lean on my mother's bureau to write study;
In a daily welcome of struggling to understand
An orient of brushed strokes incarnate in me.
Your father in you stoops to hoe and weed,
Fondles a shrub to know it grows and thrives,
A guest tended and given pride of place
As down by the Yellow River I strive to read
My tortoise shells and the seeds of invited lives
Now breed in us worlds we bend to embrace.

The opening of each part signals love in various modulations: the poet bending *lovingly* over his mother's bureau as he learns the Japanese characters for "study," 勉強, *lovely months* of reading for an autumn university examination (it was during these long months of summer study in Trinity College Dublin that my own friendship with the poet developed, in between hours in the superb college library), and the *I see you*, as his wife, Bríd, the subject of the whole of *Love Life*, is addressed. Love is there in other mentions of his mother and Bríd's father and also hidden in the *over and over* drawing of characters and *struggling to understand* them, in the *long haul* of reading for an exam, and in Bríd's gardening, nurturing *a patch slowly made your own*: these are practices of love. The sonnet that concludes the poem marries the practices of husband and wife, alternating and intertwining the drawing of characters and the tending of plants.

The poem pivots around *love's hard labour*. The work of learning is dramatically pictured in a woman in labor, her *birth struggle.* This then resonates through the rest of the poem: *Pulse and surge of insight / . . . A child born again / In the aha! of delight*, the references to parents, and the final couplet in which the characters first found drawn on tortoise shells from 2000 BC and the *seeds of invited lives* (which might be the lives of plants, of couples, of whole traditions) come together in the generative present, and *Now breed in us worlds we bend to embrace.* The other side of the labor is the joy. The second part of the poem witnesses to the delights of the life of the mind in the long-term pursuit of understanding, culminating in the testimony: *I think I'm happiest when I learn.*

There is another dimension to this poem that also connects with the Wisdom of Solomon: it is about tradition, how the past offers us worlds of meaning that can nurture the present. To reread "Study" with this in mind is to appreciate what is being passed on. There is what comes to us through our families: heirlooms reminding us of what our parents have meant to us, the skill and art of gardening, language itself—our "mother tongue." There is what we receive through our education—each academic discipline, whether in the humanities or sciences, is itself a tradition, passed on through teaching, texts, and practices. There is also the encounter with very different traditions: in his Dublin study, the poet can learn Japanese characters that give access to another civilization, and those characters themselves go back to the ancient Chinese who invented them, evoking the fascinating story of how that civilization interacted with the Japanese century after century, part of which was the Japanese adoption of Chinese signs.

Tradition sometimes has a bad name, as a "dead hand," as mere repetition, or as relying on unquestioned authority—and it can, of course, be like that. But the worst is often the corruption of the best, and here both the wisdom and the creativity of tradition at its best are suggested. To engage with earlier generations, immersed in the best of the past (and even to be able to judge what the best might be is something we slowly learn to discern with the help of wisdom from the past), can generate fresh *insight* and *illumination, moments taking flight,* new *connections made, a dawning pattern* that stretches the mind. We all, for better and for worse, inhabit traditions. Good traditions cultivate ways in which, as they are passed on, they can be critiqued, renewed, and responsively opened to new things. But the discernment needed for this is only arrived at through the long slow path of learning the tradition well. This gives the possibility of wise improvisation on it. It is what the previous chapter found in the Gospel of John and this chapter in the Wisdom of Solomon, both of which embody *love's hard labor.*

**Wisdom-Seeking between Traditions**

In a pluralistic world, most traditions that have lasted any length of time and been formative for considerable numbers of people bear many marks of their encounters with other traditions. Sometimes these are wounds still open or sensitive, sometimes there has been gain and loss, but often there have been enrichments on all sides. The ways in which cultures, civilizations, and religions interact and affect each other are endlessly diverse.

Viewed from the standpoint of a religion that is concerned about its own identity and integrity, and is in engagement with a culture or another religion, there are two extremes to which it may be drawn or forced. One is toward assimilation or even annihilation, as it meets a culture or religion that overwhelms it, fails to respect its integrity, and seduces, absorbs, or eliminates it. At the other extreme (often in reaction to fears of the first), it may attempt to live purely on its own terms, trying to reject outside influences and maintain its identity over against the surrounding culture or other religion. This may be done more defensively, by communities that simply want to live their own lives in peace, or more aggressively in order to seduce, absorb, or eliminate others.

In between these is a range of forms of engagement where most of the world's people find their identity in less extreme ways, and many of the disputes within religious communities, and between them and the nations they live in, are about which form to adopt. On each issue, decisions need to be taken. If laws are made that conflict with one's religious convictions—on military service, homosexuality, abortion, capital punishment, religious practice, the dominance of one religion, asylum-seekers, or many other matters—how should one react? Many violent conflicts involve religiously motivated violence: How does one respond to that? What should be done about religious discrimination and antireligious violence? What about equality between men and women? What form of family life is to be cultivated? In the case of marital disputes, how should they best be adjudicated? In bringing up children, how should they be taught to relate to the surrounding society—to its media, customs, dress habits, sexual mores, values, political and economic practices, and much more? Should children be educated in schools of their own religion or with everyone else in their age group—or should they be homeschooled? How should religious education be done in different sorts of schools? Should there be chaplains in schools, universities, prisons, hospitals, the military, and elsewhere—and, if so, what should they be doing? Global capitalism is both powerful and in many ways problematic, and all the religions are concerned with wealth, poverty, justice, and right livelihood: how should the religions relate to capitalism? What is the best response to the environmental challenges our world is facing, and how can religions help? The list could go on and on. Every aspect of life is in question because the major religions affect the shaping of the whole of life.

The central need on all these issues is for wise discernment and good judgment. There are many unwise, dangerous, and destructive responses to them available. The Wisdom of Solomon is passionate about wisdom because it really is essential if such questions are to be peacefully and constructively answered. Other traditions, such as Greek and other Western philosophies, Buddhism, Christianity, Islam, Hinduism, Chinese, and Japanese religions and philosophies, and secular humanisms, also demonstrate a passion for wisdom. The conclusion is obvious: *since the world desperately needs wisdom on so many issues, it would be wise for these wisdom-seeking traditions to pursue wisdom together.* This is in fact happening in many ways today. I want to give just one example that I have been involved in for about twenty years.

## From Textual Reasoning to Scriptural Reasoning

For me it began when, with my father-in-law, Daniel Hardy, I sat on the fringe of a group of young Jewish text scholars (of the Tanakh and Talmud) and philosophers (and theologians—some Jewish religious thinkers like the label "theologian," others do not) who later came to call what they were doing "Textual Reasoning." They were a fringe session, with usually between fifteen and thirty participants, at the annual meeting of the American Academy of Religion. There around ten thousand scholars and thinkers relating to the world's religions gather every year, approaching the field through most academic disciplines—theology, philosophy, history, social sciences, gender studies, regional studies, peace studies, media studies, environmental studies, natural sciences, art, literature, politics, economics, law, and the studies specifically related to each of the religious traditions.

The meetings of the group were extraordinarily stimulating. They usually had on the table (there had to be a table) texts from the Talmud (the early Rabbinic commentary on the Tanakh, the Jewish Scriptures) and texts by modern Jewish philosophers who took the Tanakh and Talmud seriously—Hermann Cohen, Franz Rosenzweig, and Emmanuel Levinas were among the favorites. Intensive concentration on the detail of the texts was combined with passionate argument about them. The conversation not only drew on both Jewish and modern academic traditions of study, scholarship, and thought but also included contemporary issues facing both Jews and the societies they live in. The intensity, the range, and the seriousness of disagreement—together with bursts of laughter—were an intoxicating mixture. It soon dawned on us Christian fringe members that we were witnessing something remarkable. This was Rabbinic Judaism being renewed and rethought for today.

Not long after the Wisdom of Solomon was written, Jews in the Roman Empire had suffered a massive trauma. The brutal Roman response to a Jewish revolt was to destroy Jerusalem and its temple in 70 CE, killing many thousands of Jews and scattering others in a diaspora across the empire and beyond. It meant the loss of key elements in their identity: the temple, the Holy Land, the holy city of Jerusalem, the sacrificial cult, and the active priesthood. Rabbinic Judaism responded to this catastrophe by reinterpreting their Scriptures, reconstituting their practices, reinventing their institutions, and reconceiving Jewish identity. It was an astonishing achievement of improvising on a tradition. The early rabbis who did this were called "the sages," "the wise ones." They worked out a pattern of Jewish understanding and practice that has continued, with many further improvisations, down to today. The North American Textual Reasoners were in this tradition.

They were acutely aware that Judaism in the twentieth century had suffered another trauma comparable to the destruction of the temple and Jerusalem: the Holocaust or, as they preferred to call it, the Shoah (Hebrew for "destruction") in which six million Jews died. They were convinced that, just as the early sages of Rabbinic Judaism recognized that the trauma they experienced necessitated a thorough reworking of their tradition, so in the aftermath of the Shoah modern Judaism needed something comparable. As I got to know them better, I found three main strands in what they were developing.

- The first was that the classic texts of premodern Judaism, especially the Tanakh and Talmud, but also liturgies, commentaries, poetry, and mystical, philosophical, historical, and other texts, had to be reread and reinterpreted today.

- The second was that the complex phenomenon of Western modernity, with all the changes it has brought, needed to be faced. The issues modernity raises need to be discussed with a view to discerning how Jews might respond to them, whether by affirming them, rejecting them, or working to transform them for the better. Among these is the Shoah, which happened in Germany, a nation that was a pioneer of modernity, not least its religion, philosophy, culture, education, science, and technology.

- The third emerged more in conversation between Christian fringe members and the Textual Reasoners. It made sense for Jews who were rereading their classic texts and at the same time facing the challenges of modernity to be in conversation with Christians and those in other religious traditions who were doing something similar. Surely, it would be worthwhile for those concerned with how one tradition could resource itself through its classics in modernity to be in conversation and argument with those concerned with a similar resourcing in other traditions.

I came to think that this integration—rereading Scriptures and other classics for their wisdom, critical and constructive engagement with modernity, and conversation and collaboration across differences and divisions—amounts to something like the DNA of wise faith for the twenty-first century.

To cut a long story short, the result of the third strand was that some of the Textual Reasoners and some Christians, joined soon afterward by some Muslims, got together to form Scriptural Reasoning. We developed a practice of reading and discussing together texts from the Tanakh, the Bible, and the Qur'an (sometimes supplemented by texts from the commentarial traditions of Judaism, Christianity, and Islam) in small groups. Through trial and error (and some painful processes), those taking part have worked out ways of studying together respectfully and fruitfully year after year.

There is now a considerable literature on Scriptural Reasoning with internet resources and regional organizations.[3] It is happening in many countries and settings, including a variety of academic and educational institutions, local congregations and synagogues, churches and mosques, prisons, hospitals, leadership courses, reconciliation and peace-building processes, civil-society organizations, and international gatherings. It has been fascinating to see how the spirit of improvisation has taken it far beyond its beginnings in unpredictable ways while remaining identifiably the same practice. I will mention just four of many examples.

### Four Improvisations—In a Convent, a Country, a Chinese University, and a Castle

#### TURVEY ABBEY

Cambridge University has regularly hosted "Open Scriptural Reasoning" evenings for those interested in tasting what it is about, some of these as part of the university's annual Festival of Ideas in which different parts of the university invite the public to share what they are thinking, discovering, and doing. One of these evenings was attended by some Benedictine nuns from

Turvey Abbey in Bedfordshire. Afterward, they got in touch to say they had very much appreciated it but wondered how it might relate to *lectio divina* (Latin for "divine reading"), the practice of group meditation on passages read aloud from the Bible that was developed in the Christian monastic tradition and that they used in their abbey.

The result some time later was that over twenty Jews, Christians, and Muslims gathered at Turvey Abbey for a day, split up into two groups, and did Scriptural Reasoning and *lectio divina* on the same texts from the Tanakh, the Bible, and the Qur'an. When we gathered together at the end of it to reflect on how it had gone, the verdict was unanimous: it worked, though everyone's experience of it was different. The participants had savored the combination and mutual illumination of a conversational, even argumentative, Jewish way of studying a text alongside a contemplative Christian way, in which there is much silence, no conversation, and concise sharing of thoughts. And for Muslims, the primacy of recitation (the meaning of "Qur'an"), speaking or reading aloud, was there in both forms, each of which had begun with listening to the text in Hebrew, Greek, or Arabic.

Three long-term practices of engagement with Scriptures had come together in a new drama of mutual understanding and wisdom-seeking.[4]

### A THOUSAND CITIES, USA

There are at least a thousand cities and towns in the United States where Jews, Christians, and Muslims read their Scriptures among themselves. The aim of A Thousand Cities is to encourage some of them to read their Scriptures together from time to time. It was conceived by Professor Peter Ochs of the University of Virginia, the principal founder of both Textual Reasoning and Scriptural Reasoning, in response to the desire by many who took part in Scriptural Reasoning to do it not only in universities and seminaries but also in all sorts of other settings.

Perhaps the most distinctive aspect of A Thousand Cities so far is the emphasis it places on learning the practice. For its first decade and more, participants learned Scriptural Reasoning by doing it in a group with those more experienced in it. But as more people wanted to take part, there was a need for a more concentrated and pedagogically informed pattern of apprenticeship. This has been developed with the help of students in the University of Virginia's doctoral program in Scriptural Reasoning, "Scripture, Interpretation, and Practice." They have even taken a bus and gone on tour with A Thousand Cities road show, stopping to give courses at places where groups gather. So, within the drama of religious traditions in engagement around their Scriptures, there is something like a drama school, where the basics can be learned.

### The Institute for Comparative Scripture and Interreligious Dialogue, Minzu University of China

Scriptural Reasoning first came to China as a result of the Archbishop of Canterbury, Rowan Williams, holding a seminar at Lambeth Palace in 2009 for Chinese academics in religious studies whom he had met during a visit to China the previous year. Yang Huilin, professor of comparative literature and religious studies at Renmin University, Beijing, responded to a paper on Scriptural Reasoning and on his return to China began a process that led in 2011 to the founding of the Institute for Comparative Scripture and Interreligious Dialogue in Minzu University of China, Beijing, under Professor You Bin. My wife, Deborah, and I visited it in October 2012.

What we found in the new institute was a radical innovation on Scriptural Reasoning. Up to now it had been Abrahamic; in Minzu, and also on the Jinan campus of Shandong University, we experienced six-text Scriptural Reasoning—on the table, besides Jewish, Christian, and Muslim texts, there were also Buddhist, Daoist, and Confucian texts on the same themes such as "suffering" or "goodness." We also noticed that the Confucian tradition acted somewhat like a *lingua franca*, providing many shared concepts and methods of interpretation as well as an etiquette of courteous conversation. In addition, the institute had integrated with Scriptural Reasoning the approach to Christian, Hindu, and Buddhist texts developed by the Harvard professor Francis Clooney, SJ, called Comparative Theology.

So not only were the Abrahamic religions joined by three more, each with deep Chinese roots, but this improvisation also brought into the act a Catholic theological engagement through reading and responding to texts of Hinduism and Buddhism. As I strained, with the help of translations and an interpreter, to follow the readings and the exchanges (it was hardest to follow the reasons for the frequent outbursts of laughter), I wondered whether I should join Micheal O'Siadhail in learning those Chinese signs.

ROSE CASTLE, CUMBRIA

In Cumbria, in the northwest of England's Lake District, Rose Castle was the residence of the Bishops of Carlisle for eight hundred years. The present bishop decided to live elsewhere, and there was strong local pressure to find for it a use in accordance with its past rather than let it become a hotel or a private home. The idea that emerged from a group led by Sarah Snyder has been to base there an international center of reconciliation. It would have four interconnected strands of activity: fostering peace and reconciliation between those in conflict or emerging from conflict, hosting and teaching Scriptural Reasoning between faiths, helping to spread religious literacy in British society and beyond, and encouraging sustainability, conservation, and care for the environment—the castle is set in an area of farming, recreation, and great natural beauty. As I write it is still at the visionary stage and may not find the funding it requires. It is an improvisation at the stage of conception, one that might enable the joint study of Scriptures to feed into better public understanding of the religions, a more peaceful world, and a better future for the natural environment.

## Five Deepenings

It is impossible to say what the future of those and other improvisations on Scriptural Reasoning will be. But, however they fare, participating in them enables something like an interfaith wisdom tradition to develop further. I would distill my own reflections on about twenty years of Scriptural Reasoning into five maxims, indicating what is desirable in such interfaith engagement at its best.

- *Go deeper into your own tradition.*

    There is nothing quite like long-term engagement with other traditions for stimulating further questioning and learning of one's own.
- *Go deeper into the traditions of others.*

    There is nothing quite like being face-to-face with others around the texts that mean most to them for gaining privileged access to what their faith and practice are really about.
- *Go deeper in your joint commitment to the common good.*

    Interreligious dialogue can be too religious, forgetting that (in the case of the Abrahamic faiths) the Creator of all is concerned with all, is good and compassionate to all, and expects believers to be likewise.
- *Go deeper into your relationships with each other.*

    One of the delightful surprises of studying Scriptures together year after year has been the quality of the collegiality

45

that has resulted, including many friendships, despite continuing deep differences on some fundamental matters.

- *Go deeper into your disagreements as well as your agreements.*

    It is good when there are agreements across differences and these can be deepened. But there are always likely to be disagreements too; it matters greatly how they are handled, whether they lead to violence, hatred, bitterness, fear, prejudice, or alienation, or whether we find ways to improve the quality of our disagreements by patient understanding, respectful argument, and generous judgment—it is possible both to be good friends and to disagree on much.

To follow such guidelines wherever they lead could enable a new act in the often tragic historical drama of Jews, Christians, and Muslims in engagement with each other and with the rest of the world.

### Within My Own Tradition: John's Drama of Learning

I attempt now to follow the first of those guidelines by taking a little further chapter 1's engagement with the Gospel of John. There, the final chapter of John was read as inspiring improvisation in the ongoing drama of living with Jesus in love. There is also in John a drama of learning, which begins in his first chapter (love is not mentioned till the third chapter).

The better-known part of that chapter is its opening eighteen verses, the prologue of the Gospel. It is a daring piece of theology that has become one of the most influential short texts in Christian thought and liturgy. As with many introductions (such as the one to this book), it was probably written (or at least completed) last. Here, it is enough to note that practically every element in it can be paralleled in the Wisdom literature and especially the Wisdom of Solomon. Even its most distinctive statement, that of incarnation (from Latin, meaning "in/into flesh"), **And the Word became flesh and lived among us, and we have seen his glory, the glory as of a father's only son, full of grace and truth** (1:14), has affinities with the personification of wisdom, her being sent by God, and her intimate partnership with Solomon (cf. Wisdom of Solomon 9:1–18). Strangely, John never names wisdom—but this may be a sign of its importance, as with not naming the mother of Jesus, the beloved disciple—or, indeed, God (as chapter 7 will discuss).

Immediately after the prologue, the lesser-known part of the chapter plunges us into the drama, and it is largely about the formation of a learning community. Two of John the Baptist's disciples (literally "learners") follow Jesus and stay with him. Andrew, one of these, brings his brother Peter, Jesus calls Philip, and Philip finds Nathanael. In this way the first learners around Jesus are gathered.

As with any worthwhile learning community, its central dynamic is questioning. The three questions in these verses are fundamental to the gospel and to the whole drama of living. The first is **"Who are you?"** (1:19, 22). It is first addressed to John the Baptist, who answers their suggestions with a repeated **"I am not"** (1:20, 21), clearing the way for a self-description as the one who points to who Jesus is. The rest of the chapter is then filled with John's and others' answers to the question, who is Jesus? Jesus, as the disciples join him, is twice addressed as **"rabbi,"** meaning "teacher" (1:38, 49). This is a teacher whose first words are a question.

This is the second question, when Jesus addresses his first learners: **"What are you looking for?"** (1:38). The verb *zetein*, to seek, search, look for, is common in the Wisdom literature for desiring and seeking wisdom—it is used three times in the first paragraph of the passage at the beginning of this chapter. Its complement verb, *heuriskein* or *heurein*, "to find," is also there twice, and five times in John 1:42–46. Both words recur throughout John's Gospel. The final *zetein* is married to the who question when the risen Jesus asks Mary Magdalene: **"Whom are you looking for?"** When Jesus calls her **"Mary!"** she replies: **"Rabbouni!" (which means Teacher)** (20:15–16).

The third question, the first words addressed to Jesus, is **"Rabbi" (which translated means Teacher), "where are you staying?"** (1:38). The verb *menein*, meaning "stay," "remain," "continue," or "abide," has already been noted (in chapter 1) as a key term in John, with levels of meaning, ranging from Jesus's lodging, through the dwelling of Wisdom, to **close to the Father's heart** (1:18). Its sense of long-term mutuality and sharing of life and love as well as wisdom opens up a vision of the wisdom-seeking community of love.

Sharon Ringe's lovely little book on John's understanding of Jesus Christ and Christian community is called *Wisdom's Friends*.[5] She shows how wisdom and friendship come together in identifying both who Jesus is and what the community around him is about. One answer to all three questions is, therefore, Jesus is the wise friend who meets the desire of others for a life of abiding, wise friendship. She also shows how wisdom and friendship resonate and inspire action across the alienating divisions both of John's world and of ours—her contemporary example is of Latin American Christian communities that challenge divisions of wealth, power, class, and race. The interfaith wisdom of the five deepenings proposed above could be another example, since the five actually pivot around the fourth, the deepening of relationships with each other through wisdom-seeking friendships.

It is to such friendships and other face-to-face relationships that we now turn.

3

# Face-to-Face

*The Heart of Life's Drama*

A large part of the power of film is that it gives us access to face-to-face encounters of so many kinds. We all have our favorites, those we remember and replay. Among mine is Richard Attenborough's *Gandhi*, especially when Gandhi leads the salt march and is confronted by British soldiers—there is a close-up of his calm face just before he is brutally beaten. In *The Lord of the Rings*, I think of the scene near the end of the third part when the ring has been destroyed, Frodo has been rescued, wakes up in bed, and is reunited with one after another of those to whom he has become so close. In *The Remains of the Day*, there is the exquisitely portrayed relationship between the characters played by Anthony Hopkins and Emma Thompson, so much of it conveyed through their facial expressions. In *Of Gods and Men*, the story of a monastery in Algeria, most of whose monks were killed, the last meal of the monks as they await their fate, listening to *Swan Lake*, and looking from face to face, is one of the most moving encounters I know. In the theater, there is the further dimension of being "live," though it lacks (or, perhaps, is made more precious and lifelike by) film's capacity to be replayed at will. The face-to-face between actors on stage is enhanced by the dynamics between them and the audience. I was once present at a performance of Shakespeare's "Macbeth" by Mark Rylance and his company in Broadmoor, a top-security psychiatric hospital. Many in the audience had, like Macbeth, committed murders. I knew the play well but had never experienced it like this, sitting among that audience. Then at the end of the play, Rylance and all his company turned to face the audience and engage in a discussion, so there was new, unrehearsed dialogue as the patients expressed their responses.

The main reason for the popularity and impact of film and theater is that they resonate so widely and deeply with the face-to-face dramas of our ordinary lives. Micheal O'Siadhail describes a common airport scene in "Transit":

> Urgencies of language: check-in, stand-by, take-off.
> Everything apace, businesslike. But I'm happy here
> Gazing at all the meetings and farewells. I love
> To see those strangers' faces quickened and bare.
> A lost arrival is wandering. A moment on edge,
> He pans a lounge for his countersign of welcome.
> A flash of greeting, sudden lightening of baggage,
> As though he journeyed out only to journey home.
> I watch a parting couple in their embrace and freeing.
> The woman turns, a Veronica with her handkerchief
> Absorbing into herself a last stain of a countenance.
> She dissolves in crowds. An aura of her leaving glance
> Travels through the yearning air. Tell me we live
> For those faces wiped into the folds of our being.[1]

The final sentence suggests why the face-to-face is so fundamental to who we are. Much research has been done on the bonding of mothers and babies and the importance of their face-to-face interaction. Our early formation with parents, brothers, sisters, wider family, playmates, and others shapes us profoundly—those faces are *wiped into the folds of our being.* So too, as we go through life, are faces of teachers, lovers, friends, enemies, colleagues, and so on, and the media, not least Facebook and similar websites, give us countless more. Much of our interior life of memory, thought, and imagination is a traffic in images of interactions with other people as we remember aspects of our past and present relationships or rehearse for the future. Certain faces become iconic for us, for better or worse. And the corruption of the best is the worst: we can be haunted, even traumatized all over again, by faces and what they recall.

I have been fascinated for decades by the central importance of the face-to-face and also by how many ways there are of getting it right or wrong. I am also convinced of the great importance of the images and concepts we use to think, imagine, form judgments, and make decisions. The search for wisdom in the drama of living is greatly helped if we think with fruitful images and concepts. The "face-to-face" can be taken as both an image and a concept or idea—what literary critics call a "trope," a turn of speech that concentrates and improvises on meaning. It points to a core feature of human life, and to reflect on it helps to make more sense of the drama of living.

The idea of the face-to-face has for me been like a large container into which further meaning has been poured over the years—sometimes drop by drop, sometimes flooding in. This chapter will do two things.

First, it will trace some of the sources of that abundant meaning that I have discovered over the years. It will follow my autobiography through some pivotal moments of illumination, from schoolboy acting, through learning from a formative teacher and being gripped by a Jewish philosopher, to the current immersion in the Gospel of John and fascination by its drama. The hope is that this might help readers to enrich and deepen their own conception of the face-to-face—a fruitful image/concept/trope ideally allows many people to improvise on it from their own experience.

Second, I will focus on one example that embodies many of the elements I find most significant, the international federation of L'Arche communities where those with and without severe learning disabilities live together. This too will be approached autobiographically through the recollection of a memorable ten-day retreat in France at the mother community of the federation, led by the founder of L'Arche, Jean Vanier. The main topic of the retreat was the second half of the Gospel of John, and Vanier's meditations and his commentary on John led into intense mutual illumination of the Gospel and L'Arche. L'Arche can be seen as a creative contemporary improvisation on the Gospel, offering a prophetic sign of love and hope for the twenty-first century, symbolized in its practice of footwashing.

## The "Face-to-Face"—Gathering Meaning

I think it was through acting in ancient Greek plays in school that I first began to stand back a little from just being involved in face-to-face living in the usual ways in order to reflect on what it might mean and how important it is. Acting in a comedy by Aristophanes or a tragedy by Sophocles meant wearing a mask, as the Greeks did in their performances. A good deal has been written about how powerful the interaction of masked figures can be in such drama and their expressiveness despite the fixity of the mask. But for me as a schoolboy what made the greatest impression was taking on another identity, wearing the mask for long periods, and then taking it off and having very different face-to-face engagements. The entry into another form of face-to-face somehow intensified the ordinary experience of it.

### "Middle Distance" Realism

It was a good deal later, after studying classics and theology for some years, that the next key stage in reflection came, stimulated by two sources that have continued to be generative up to the present.

The first was the theologian Hans Frei. When I arrived at Yale and asked to take a course of his, he told me he was not teaching it that year, but he offered to give it to me one-to-one. This amazing generosity provided a face-to-face setting in which some of his own fundamental thinking could be communicated and explored. Central to his concerns at the time was "realistic narrative," the sort of storytelling that, for example, includes much of the Bible, and all the Gospels, together with most of the classic English and Russian novels by Jane Austen, George Eliot, Leo Tolstoy, or Fyodor Dostoyevsky.

Realistic narratives tell of reality through characters and events in interaction over time. They have a primary perspective on life: what happens between people, the things they do and say, the ways they think about and imagine each other, the development of lives and groups over time. Besides this main perspective, others are possible, moving in two different directions.

### Wide-Angle Overview

First, in the direction of a broader, more general perspective, it is possible to take a "big picture," "wide-angle" view of life. This attempts some sort of overview. It is not about the interplay of specific people but about the wide horizon within which those interactions happen. There always is such a broad framework, but Frei's point is that in the Gospels or in Eliot's *Middlemarch*, it is not dominant in the sense that the stories are only illustrations of it. Rather, the stories are the heart of the matter, and the most important meanings are conveyed through characters and their interactions, not through general statements.

In the Gospels, the horizon is God and the whole of creation, but this is not mainly conveyed through abstract concepts, an overarching story, a philosophical framework, or a systematic theology. Rather, who God is and the meaning of creation are primarily given through the story of Jesus, his disciples, his opponents, and others he meets, as well as what happens to them and between them. To appreciate this reality more, we have to return again and again to the story. We do need concepts and frameworks, but the main way of judging them is whether they are in line with the testimony in stories, not the other way around. Christianity has been found to be compatible with many philosophies, worldviews, ethical practices, and political programs (often transforming them in the process of adopting them), and these have contributed to its persuasiveness, plausibility, and proliferation, but at its heart is a Person and his relations with other people, portrayed primarily through a story in realistic narrative form.

### Ordinary Face-to-Face

I love the ending of *Middlemarch*, in which George Eliot sums up the perspective of a worldview centered on this sort of realism as embodied in the ordinary life of her fictional town:

> Sir James never ceased to regard Dorothea's second marriage as a mistake; and indeed this remained the tradition concerning it in Middlemarch, where she was spoken of to a younger generation as a fine girl who married a sickly clergyman, old enough to be her father, and in little more than a year after his death

gave up her estate to marry his cousin—young enough to have been his son, with no property, and not well-born. Those who had not seen anything of Dorothea usually observed that she could not have been "a nice woman," else she would not have married either the one or the other.

Certainly those determining acts of her life were not ideally beautiful. They were the mixed result of young and noble impulse struggling amidst the conditions of an imperfect social state, in which great feelings will often take the aspect of error, and great faith the aspect of illusion. For there is no creature whose inward being is so strong that it is not greatly determined by what lies outside it. A new Theresa will hardly have the opportunity of reforming a conventual life, any more than a new Antigone will spend her heroic piety in daring all for the sake of a brother's burial: the medium in which their ardent deeds took shape is forever gone. But we insignificant people with our daily words and acts are preparing the lives of many Dorotheas, some of which may present a far sadder sacrifice than that of the Dorothea whose story we know.

Her finely touched spirit had still its fine issues, though they were not widely visible. Her full nature, like that river of which Cyrus broke the strength, spent itself in channels which had no great name on the earth. But the effect of her being on those around her was incalculably diffusive: for the growing good of the world is partly dependent on unhistoric acts; and that things are not so ill with you and me as they might have been, is half owing to the number who lived faithfully a hidden life, and rest in unvisited tombs.

That vision of the importance of "our daily words and acts," being content with having "no great name on the earth," and living "faithfully a hidden life" is at the heart of a gospel-shaped worldview. Eliot had reacted against her early Protestant Christian commitment to become (perhaps—she did not wear her heart on her sleeve) a deeply ethical agnostic. But, whatever her framework, one may appreciate the extraordinary wisdom of her novels. One of the things Hans Frei taught was the value of such wisdom, whether set within a Christian theology or not, and he learned a great deal from literature and democratic politics.

### Interiority—Inside View

Instead of moving toward the "macro" broad framework and wide-angle view, one can go in the opposite direction toward the "micro" and emphasize human interiority: what goes on inside individuals, in their thoughts, feelings, fantasies, subconscious, or stream of consciousness. Like the other extreme of the big picture, this too is important. *Middlemarch* has many insightful descriptions of what is going on inside its varied cast of characters. But the primary perspective is the interactions between them, and most of what goes on in their hearts and heads is in fact about this interplay. Indeed, the strange effect of an "omniscient author," who has access to her characters' interior lives, is to realize all the more clearly that in our ordinary lives, outside of such fiction, none of us has such an overview, and we would be wise to be very cautious in our general conclusions even about those we know best, let alone those we know less well or humanity as a whole. The ironic humor of Eliot about Middlemarch's public opinion of Dorothea, which "usually observed that she could not have been 'a nice woman'" is just the final example of her habitual appreciation of the limitation, misconception, and obscurity that are part of our knowledge of each other. The omniscient author can know, but in real life we have to observe, guess, interpret, act, and react. Without the privileged access of an author of fiction, we have to ask each other questions and listen attentively to what is said and hinted and be alert for nonverbal signals.

In the Gospels, we learn very little about the interiority of Jesus or others—the New Testament character that we can have most insight into is Paul because of his own testimony in letters.

This does not mean that what goes on inside us is unimportant for the Gospels—the "heart," "soul," "spirit," or "mind" of a person is a place of thought, faith and trust, deceit, good and bad desire, discernment, temptation, judgment, decision, prayer, and much else. But the crucial orientation of all this is toward life with others before God. Just as there are novels that center on interiority and streams of consciousness, so there are spiritualities that are mainly about the cultivation of inner states and experiences. In these, the balance has shifted away from the primary orientation of realistic narrative.

The Gospels make it clear that for Jesus and for his followers the point of living is loving. This is not primarily about introspection or self-cultivation but about long-term committed relationships in community, accompanied by other relationships (even with enemies) marked by love, justice, compassion, forgiveness, and generosity. Just as the gospel can be, and has been, related positively to many philosophies, worldviews, and systems of thought and practice, so it can and does relate to many forms of interiority, spiritual discipline, meditative practices, self-cultivation, and habits of thought, feeling, or imagination. The test is, do these serve the love of God and neighbor?

Studying with Hans Frei led me into a doctoral dissertation on how the twentieth-century Swiss theologian Karl Barth interpreted the realistic narratives of the Gospels. In the course of that, I came upon one of the most perceptive books that I know about the literary side of this, J. P. Stern's *On Realism*.[2] It gave the concept that for me best sums up the approach of realistic narrative: the "middle distance" perspective in which primacy is given to people and events in interaction over time and not to their interiority or to large abstract systems or general frameworks.

Micheal O'Siadhail later wrote a poem called "Perspective," which drew on the language of painting and film to make the sort of points I have been suggesting above. It includes sections called "Wide Angle" and "Close-up," and the following one named "Middle Distance":

> We learn the touch-and-go of being
> Between, figures in a half-distance,
> Neither a loom too close to view
> Or a shape so vague as not to matter;
> Rather brokers in the thick of things,
> Movers in a loose focus of betwixtness
> We walk a canvas's middle ground.[3]

### Before the Face of the Other

The second rich source that I discovered in Yale was Emmanuel Levinas, whose philosophy of the face gripped me. The connection with Frei's realistic narrative was obvious (though in fact I did not see it for many years): the middle distance is the perspective in which we actually see faces—too close up and they blur or we see only a nose, lips, or an eye; too far away and we do not see faces at all, just a big picture without particular persons.

I was introduced to Levinas through a course on "Ministry as Hospitality" taught by Henri Nouwen, a Dutch Catholic priest who later became well known for his writing on spirituality, and who lived the last period of his life in a L'Arche community in Toronto. Talking with him about my course essay, he suggested reading Levinas, of whom I had never heard (he too was to become much better known). Levinas was a Lithuanian Jew who lived most of his life in France and only late in life was recognized as a major philosopher and given a professorship in the Sorbonne. He had been interned by the German army during the Second World War (interned rather than killed, since he was a soldier in the French army) and lost many family members in the Shoah. These experiences led him to rethink philosophy, and above all, ethics.

The book Nouwen recommended, *Totality and Infinity*, was like no other I had ever read. It was both rigorously conceptual and poetic at the same time, its dense prose needing to be read and reread—and even after many readings I felt there was far more to be found. Yet "difficult" was not really the right description; it was more a matter of superabundant meaning that went far beyond "interesting ideas" and constantly confronted me with a radical ethical challenge. Here was philosophy born out of moral passion. Its central point was simple: before the face of another person I am radically responsible. The face of the other is not just another element in my world. It interrupts my world with an appeal for justice and compassion. The "appeal in the face of the other" cries out to me to be responsible. Above all, its message is, Thou shalt not kill! The relevance of this to Nouwen's course on hospitality was that one of Levinas's many rich images/concepts/tropes is "the hospitality of the face": in facing another we are summoned to welcome him or her and above all to welcome the stranger, the outsider, the one in most need.

Levinas is devastatingly critical of what he calls "totality," which connects with what I have been calling frameworks, systems, overviews. There is no overview of you facing me. I do not have one, and you do not have one. We rely on each other interacting—speaking, gesturing, or acting. Even less does a third person have a privileged vantage point; on the contrary, what happens between you and me, as we look into each other's eyes, is unique, a dynamic of summons and response that cannot be fitted into any system or other totality, or grasped through a third party's gaze. Levinas finds "totality" pervading Western thought, as thinkers try to take the third person standpoint and so view reality as a whole in order to arrive at a dominant, controlling overview. This way of thinking finds its way into religion, politics, management, education, and other spheres; its extremes include the totalitarianisms of Nazis and Communists. It is there in capitalists who see markets and bottom lines, not faces, and in religious believers who claim a God's-eye view. Resisting it is the "infinity" of the face-to-face ethical relationship that cannot be contained in a totality.

O'Siadhail has time and again taken up this theme. In "Après Vous Monsieur!," which has the dedication *"For Emmanuel Levinas, philosopher; born January 12th 1906, died Christmas Day 1995,"* he refers to Levinas's later radicalizing still further of his ethic through taking responsibility even for the other's exercise of responsibility:

> No "because," just infinite command,
> a face hiding more than it will show
> calls you hostage and brother's keeper,
> keeper even of your keeping me.

The last lines of that poem go simply to the heart of the matter:

> An outsider turns his insistent face.
> Stranger, come in.[4]

Elsewhere, O'Siadhail complements facing the stranger with facing our most intimate others, and he addresses his wife:

> In the strange openness of your face, I'm powerless.
> Always this love. Always this infinity between us.[5]

Levinas gave me an enduring suspicion of overviews and generalizations (while still acknowledging their usefulness and unavoidability) and a fascination with the face and facing. He was also my introduction to modern Jewish philosophy. For more than twenty years, I read him in private in an English academic setting largely hostile to him and other continental European philosophers. I vividly remember the scornful, confident dismissal of Levinas by a leading English philosopher when, as a young lecturer in Birmingham, I tentatively put forward some of his ideas in a discussion group. Then I encountered the Jewish philosophers in the Textual Reasoning group described in the previous chapter. Several knew Levinas far better than I, and, at least as important, actually practiced "the hospitality of the face." Conversation with them gave me the confidence finally to write about him.

Years previously, I had had a formative collaboration with a colleague in Birmingham University, Frances Young, on Paul's second letter to the Corinthians.[6] Her book on being the mother of a severely disabled son, Arthur, was called *Face to Face*.[7] In our conversations and seminars on the letter, two key verses centered on the face:

> And all of us, with unveiled faces, seeing the glory of the Lord as though reflected in a mirror, are being transformed into the same image from one degree of glory to another; for this comes from the Lord, the Spirit. . . . For it is the God who said, "Let light shine out of darkness," who has shone in our hearts to give the light of the knowledge of the glory of God in the face of Jesus Christ. (2 Cor. 3:18; 4:6)

How might Levinas's philosophy of the face relate to Paul's conception of a community of people in whose hearts is **the light of the knowledge of the glory of God in the face of Jesus Christ?** "Living before the face of Jesus Christ" became one of my main ways of conceiving Christian faith, uniting the elements in those verses: the community, **all of us;** our ongoing experience of **being transformed in the Spirit;** the horizon of the whole of reality, created by **the God who said, "Let light shine out of darkness";** the mind-stretching **knowledge of the glory** of God; and the interiority **in our hearts** of **the face of Jesus Christ.** That has the "wide-angle" perspective of God and all creation, and it also has the inner life of our hearts. But Paul's central concern is for those to come together in the ongoing life of a face-to-face community centered on Jesus Christ, who is identified through the story of his birth, ministry, Last Supper, death, and resurrection. The "middle distance" perspective is primary both for Paul's relationship with the Corinthians and for identifying Jesus Christ.

The eventual written outcome of years of engagement with Levinas, Textual Reasoning, 2 Corinthians, and much else was a book that tried to explore the face and facing from many angles.[8] But the face-to-face was more than just a topic for reflection in the book. Even though we obviously cannot have two-way exchanges with authors who are dead or absent, it is possible to extend the ethos of Levinas's face-to-face to "conversations" with texts, and the book tried to do that. But still to come was a further image/concept/trope that could draw together conversation, realistic narrative, and the face-to-face more satisfactorily than any other.

### Drama and the Gospel of John

This concept was drama. For me, it had been something like the ignored "elephant in the room." Many theologians and other thinkers have found it illuminating, both as a concept and through reflecting on theater, opera, film, television, and other media. More widely, drama, together with the images and ideas associated with it, is one of the most common sets of descriptive terms in our culture—think of role, cast, actor, character, stage, off-stage, director, producer, script, plot, set, props, cue, prompt, play, tragedy, comedy, interlude, farce, pantomime, monologue, dialogue, act, scene, performance, curtain, scenery, costume, mime, chorus, antagonist, rehearse. It rather slowly dawned on me how fruitful drama could be for integrating and taking further themes I had been developing over many years.

Drama (I am taking Shakespeare's plays as a norm) takes a primarily middle-distance perspective, with people in face-to-face interaction. It presents the immediacy of life being lived now, giving a sense of openness to the future as it unfolds through what the actors say and do. There can be interiority through monologues and soliloquies, but these have to play their part in the human interactions. There can be a framework of meaning (though it is instructive how difficult it has been for scholars and others to agree on what Shakespeare's might have been— O'Siadhail describes Shakespeare's self-concealment, addressing him as *Greatest mirror, most hidden holder up*),[9] but the meaning is primarily communicated through the characters in interplay, not through general statements.

I have found this perspective especially illuminating in a current project, an interpretation of the Gospel of John. Approaching it, I was somewhat uneasy with some theological approaches, both ancient and modern. They often seemed to lose sight of the fact that John spends most of his time on the story, told in a series of dramatic episodes. They drew from the Gospel much teaching, especially on God, Jesus Christ, the Holy Spirit, discipleship, Christian community, and the ethics of love. Much of this was illuminating and gave food for thought, prayer, and living. But it often missed out on the way most of this is taught through dramatic narrative, requiring constant rereading of the narrative to keep it fresh. The statements of doctrine easily become an endpoint of teaching rather than a stimulus to return again and again to drink from their source. Further, the purpose of John is to enable participation in the ongoing drama of loving and living with Jesus, and this requires that doctrine be continually rethought in relation both to the story of Jesus's life, death, and resurrection and to its continuation in the community of his friends and followers. Another way of putting these problems is that one tendency of doctrine is to paint a big picture that runs the danger of losing touch with the "middle distance" of people and events in interaction through time.

I was also uneasy with some forms of spirituality based on John. These rightly explore the potential for meditation and contemplation on the rich symbols of light and darkness, water, wine and vine, wind, bread, seeds, shepherd, and more. They also rightly make much of the intimacy of the mutual indwelling of Jesus, his Father, and his disciples—and of the Spirit Jesus breathes into each. But again there was a danger of missing something of the dynamic of the drama, of concentrating on the transformation of interiority, and losing out on following, building community, prophetic witnessing, doing **greater works** (14:12), and improvising on the drama in line with Jesus's words as he breathed the Holy Spirit on his disciples: **As the Father has sent me, so I send you** (20:21).

So much for the negative side. The more I read John bearing in mind the perspectives discussed above, the more I appreciated how he performed something of a *tour de force* of dramatic presentation that integrates both the other perspectives under the sign of love.

His big picture is best seen in his prologue, beginning with God and all creation in its first verse, and culminating in its last verse with the Son **close to the Father's heart** (1:18). This unites an unsurpassable framework with intimacy. But in between those verses is utter immersion in the drama of history, its light and darkness, the witness of John, the rejection and reception of Jesus, the community of believers, the law of Moses, and, above all, the Word becoming flesh and living among us.

The interiority, combined with a further development of the prologue's big picture, is seen in the climax of Jesus's life in the Farewell Discourse on the night before he died (chapters 13–17).

The conversation with his disciples culminates in Jesus praying in intimate conversation with his Father (chapter 17). This is a rare glimpse of what being **close to the Father's heart** might mean. It has the richest statements of mutual indwelling: **"As you, Father, are in me and I am in you, may they also be in us"** (17:21), and **"The glory that you have given me I have given them, so that they may be one, as we are one, I in them and you in me, that they may become completely one"** (17:22–23). It is also framed by evoking the time-encompassing presence of God: pictures of Jesus in the presence of his Father **before the world existed** (17:5) and later in that same presence with those he loves (17:24). Both the evocations of God's presence and the interiority of prayer and mutual indwelling are centered on the "middle distance" of loving; indeed, they might be seen as John's way of saying that ultimately there is only this eternal love life. And throughout this prayer there is repeated insistence that the central concern of Jesus is for the continuing drama in the world. The two incomplete verses just quoted continue: **"so that the world may believe that you have sent me"** (v. 21), and **"so that the world may know that you have sent me and have loved them even as you have loved me"** (v. 23). The good of the world, the sending of Jesus to it, and the approaching final act of the drama in Jesus's death and resurrection have their goal in love: **"so that the love with which you have loved me may be in them, and I in them"** (17:26). There is a life of love embracing an interiority of love within a framework of the love of God, and both love and God are primarily defined by who Jesus is as the main character of this drama.

So the Gospel of John has poured the latest flood of meaning into the image/concept/trope of the face-to-face. But, as previous chapters have made clear, this is a Gospel that is not adequately understood unless it is improvised on, with the Holy Spirit inspiring **greater works** and leading into more and more truth through a life of love. It is an open-ended Gospel that invites into ever-fresh loving. I want to explore just one example of this that I consider prophetic for the twenty-first century.

### L'Arche—Sign of Love and Community

*Magnifique! . . . A deepening in St John's Gospel. Personal transformation. Life-giving. Well organized. . . . Nourishing, inviting, lots of laughter, rich and deep interactions. . . . Great to have space and time with Jean, on John, to have the prayer and the group sharing. . . . Full and rich—the word, the group, the place, space, liturgy and music, being in Trosly. . . . All I hoped for and more.*

Those were some of the comments given in feedback about the overall experience of a ten-day retreat in Trosly-Breuil in France in February 2012. The thirty participants from many countries were all involved in various roles in L'Arche communities. In these communities (now well over one hundred on all continents), people with and without learning disabilities live together. Several on the retreat had lived in such communities for more than twenty years; most had more than ten years experience with L'Arche. The main topic was chapters 13–21 of the Gospel of John, and every morning Jean Vanier, founder of L'Arche, meditated aloud on a chapter, followed by discussion. The specific feedback on his sessions included the following:

> Wise, thoughtful, evocative. Full of humor . . . he continues to surprise and inspire me. . . . He opens windows in my heart . . . an invitation to dwell more fully in this Gospel . . . he has made each encounter and each passage come alive.

My wife, Deborah, and I were privileged to be on this retreat. For me, it was a culmination of being involved for more than twenty years with L'Arche, never as a resident in community, but in other ways such as theological accompaniment, consultation, larger and smaller gatherings, pilgrimages, visits to communities, writing projects, friendships, and at present an initiative by Deborah exploring how a L'Arche project might be developed in Cambridge. For me, the retreat gave further insight into the character and significance of L'Arche.

*Five Vital Strands*

At least five main strands came together.

1. There was Jean Vanier as founder of L'Arche, telling many stories and drawing on the wisdom distilled through the nearly fifty years of its existence.[10] They were mostly stories of people with disabilities, of the assistants who have lived with them, and of the transformations (and resistance to transformation) that he has witnessed, but also some about the development of L'Arche itself from one household in Trosly to an international federation. Such testimonies indicate the heart of L'Arche: people with and without severe learning disabilities sharing life together in ways that are not about one set "doing good to" the other but about deep mutuality, often resulting in surprising friendships.

2. Inextricable from that was Vanier's interpretation of the Gospel of John, whose roots in him go back even more than fifty years. Of all the books on this Gospel that at present are piled high in my study as I work on a commentary, Vanier's meditative commentary, *Drawn into the Mystery of Jesus through the Gospel of John*,[11] stands out. It is an exploration both of the "deep plain sense" of John and of the meaning of L'Arche.

   I wrote some years ago about this mutual illumination of John and L'Arche in Vanier's writing,[12] and those conclusions have been confirmed and expanded by further involvement with L'Arche and work on John. Jesus performs what John calls "signs" in order to embody his message of abundant life. L'Arche might be seen as improvising further life-giving signs.

As Vanier meditates on John, time and again there are resonances between the Gospel's signs and what goes on in L'Arche communities. They are places of celebration, and Vanier makes much of the fact that the first sign Jesus does is to provide a huge amount of wine for a wedding:

> Jesus is celebrating because a wedding is a celebration
> of love.
> And Jesus has come to reveal, strengthen and deepen
> love. . . .
> God loves us abundantly
> And wants to give us more and more life and joy.[13]

They are places where, as for those in Jesus's healing signs,

> each person, whatever his or her abilities or disabilities,
> is unique and important;
> each one is a child of God, loved by God. . . .
> Our communities are not a "solution" for all people
> with disabilities;
> they can only be a sign that those we welcome are
> important
> —so all are important. . . .
> When the weak and strong come together in mutual
> friendship,
> they bridge the gap and become bonded together
> In a common humanity.[14]

3. On the retreat were L'Arche people from around the world, each with a rich experience of community, but nobody with any illusions about the difficulties, challenges, and anguish inseparable from it. Above all, there was a sense of their rootedness in ordinary "family" life, from the celebration of birthdays (and many other occasions—"we never let

an opportunity slip by without at least singing and prefer-
ably a cake") to the wiping of bottoms. It is described by
Micheal O'Siadhail in his poem dedicated to Jean Vanier,
"Admiral of Arks," which we read together:

> Slobber of dailyness. Tasks begun and rebegun.
> Small humdrum of the wounded,
> Seizures, tears, rushes of anger or affection.
>
> More listening than wanting to do things for,
> Fecundity of nothing accomplished,
> Ordinary unhurried to and fro of rapport.
>
> No mask or echelons, a kind of upside-downness,
> Osmosis of bare and broken
> Takers and givers in a single fragile caress. [15]

4. The retreat was also a community of faith. Everyone was
   Christian, from many denominations, with Catholics
   the largest single group, and we had liturgies in several
   traditions, small faith-sharing groups, silent prayer, and
   time for individual prayer. L'Arche has people from many
   faiths and none, and its approach has something of the
   ethos of "multiple deepening" and friendship described
   in the previous chapter. For example, on a visit to Trosly
   a few months earlier, I had met with a group of Muslim
   members of L'Arche who were having a consultation with
   Muslim scholars from Al-Azhar University in Egypt and a
   Christian scholar of Islam, exploring together a Muslim
   theology and spirituality for L'Arche. Some years previously, Deborah and I had visited Asha Niketan, the L'Arche
   in Chennai (Madras) in southern India, whose leader was
   Hindu and whose members were Hindu, Muslim, and
   Christian.

   This retreat, most of whose participants were experienced, mature Christians, was a time when there could be
   wisdom-seeking about some of the difficult and complex

questions of faith, and the theme during the afternoons of the second week was "Accompanying the Dying" (I will take this up in chapter 6). So it was something like a model of what the church can be at its best: a fellowship of prayer, friendship, learning, and practice, committed to working out with others God's purposes in the drama of living.

5. Organizational issues were part of the wisdom-seeking. Conversations revealed a realism born out of many years of community-building in different countries. Bearing responsibility for vulnerable people over the long-term requires as good an organization as possible and careful attention to "succession"—how continuity and creativity across the generations can be sustained. L'Arche had just been through a discernment process over some years, involving all its communities, their management boards and supporters, focused first on its "identity and mission" and then on "community and belonging." That had gone with agreeing on a new constitution for its international federation of communities, and one of the newly elected international coordinators, Eileen Glass from Australia, took part in the retreat.

During those years of joint discernment and constitutional reform, Vanier had gradually withdrawn from all leadership roles, and I am fascinated by the way the Gospel of John has shaped his approach to his own succession. Most scholars agree that John was written partly in order to enable a good transition across generations. Jesus says, "**It is to your advantage that I go away**," and promises that his followers, inspired by the Holy Spirit, will do even "**greater works**" (14:12) after him. Here in the retreat, Vanier was sharing the secret of succession by drawing people deeper into the Gospel of John, encouraging them to become "wise in the Spirit" as they approach succession in local communities, regional organizations, and the international federation.

Each of those five strands is woven together with the others: the friendships enabled in L'Arche connect with John, with the dailyness of living together, with the fellowship of faith, and with the need for organization.

## Face-to-Feet

On the last evening of the retreat, we washed each other's feet as part of a L'Arche liturgy based on John 13. In his commentary, Vanier introduces this scene as follows:

> Jesus kneels
> at the feet of his disciples;
> as a slave,
> he washes their feet.
>
> In this simple gesture
> he reveals the face of God
> and a new way for us
> to exercise authority
> to bring people to unity
> and to work for peace.
>
> This is the way of humility
> and service.[16]

Against the compulsions of power, the echelons, the pyramid structure of much authority, and the admiration of strong, invulnerable success, Vanier says, "Service to the little ones gives the way to change the world." It is *a kind of upside-downness* (O'Siadhail—Vanier uses the French *bouleversement*), giving dignity to each one, a compassionate conscience to the exercise of power and authority, and a new model of society—instead of a pyramid, a body

> where each and every person has a place,
> whatever their abilities or disabilities,

71

where each one is dependent on the other. . . .
Jesus, revealing himself as the least one in society,
the one who does the dirty jobs,
the one who is in the last place,
calls his followers to be attentive to the least in society.[17]

This "face-to-feet" is a beatitude, a way of being blessed by God: **"For I have set you an example, that you also should do as I have done to you. . . . If you know these things, you are blessed if you do them"** (John 13:15, 17). It is a blessing whose sign is given one-to-one through the tenderness of touch. Vanier tells the story of Eric:

To wash a person's feet
is a gesture that creates and expresses a communion of
    hearts.
I became more aware of the importance of this gesture
when I left the leadership of my community
and lived a sabbatical year in one of our homes
that welcomes people with severe handicaps.
Among them was Eric.
We had met him at the local psychiatric hospital.
When he arrived he was a young lad of sixteen:
he was blind, deaf and could not walk or speak.
He was not toilet trained.
I have never seen so much anguish in a young person as
    I saw in Eric.
There was a desire in him to die;
he just would not keep down food in his stomach.

Many of those with disabilities
who are welcomed in our L'Arche communities
have a broken self-image.
They have been seen as a disappointment for their
    parents;
they are not wanted as they are,

so they feel they are no good.
If people are not loved,
they can feel that they are in fact not loveable,
that they are somehow bad or evil.
Our hope in welcoming such people
is to help them to transform their broken or negative
    self-image
into a positive one and find self-esteem.
The vision of L'Arche is to help people rediscover their
    value,
their beauty, their importance.
Only then can they begin to grow and do beautiful
    things;
they respond to love with love.
Someone who has a negative self-image will only want
    to do
negative things to themselves or to others.

But how could we help Eric make this transformation
when he could neither see nor hear nor understand?
The only way to communicate with him was through
    touch.
Through the way we touched, held and washed his body
with respect and love,
we were able to communicate and reveal to him
that he was precious.[18]

To be face-to-face with Jesus is to be invited to imitate him
in gentleness, humility, and doing the dirty jobs, and to follow
his gaze toward those like Eric who seem least important.

### A Sign for the Twenty-First Century

Would Eric have been known by name as someone of "value,
beauty and importance" in any previous period of history?
Through the now considerable literature on L'Arche, together

with websites, videos, and other media, the names of many people with such disabilities are known, and they are seen to have played a major role in shaping their communities. And since these communities embody qualities such as love, compassion, joy, gentleness, wisdom, service, humor, and abundant life, it is evident that they have helped to achieve something that is both utterly extraordinary and has great potential for humanity's future. Most people would want a community with such qualities to be part of their own and their children's lives. To acknowledge the indispensability of people with severe disabilities to the flourishing of these communities is to grasp something counterintuitive, momentous, and true—analogous to Copernicus discovering that the earth goes around the sun. Vanier writes:

> I must say that for myself it has been a transformation
> to be in L'Arche.
> When I founded L'Arche it was to "be good" and to "do
> good"
> to people with disabilities.
> I had no idea how these people were going to do good
> to me!
> A bishop once told me:
> "You in L'Arche are responsible for a Copernican
> revolution:
> up until now we used to say that we should do good to
> the poor.
> You are saying that the poor are doing good to you!"[19]

So instead of the rich, able, powerful, and invulnerable being central, in this new world if we want to be blessed we stay close to the poor, disabled, vulnerable, and those who do menial work. The blessing happens where dirty feet are being washed amid the *slobber of dailyness.* To stay close to them (I write as one who is at present relatively rich and able) can be transformative for us, for them, and for society. Above all, this happens through

74

enabling a community of love, joy, tenderness, and discernment. Of course, they do not shape communities by themselves. The very dependence of those with disabilities ensures that they have to be in community with others who can help them, in a partnership of the weaker and the stronger. And it is those "face-to-face" communities that are also "face-to-feet," which hold the secret of God's future for us:

> The history of humanity has changed
> since God knelt humbly at our feet, begging our love.[20]

# 4

# Rereading and Rehearsing

*Classic Surprises*

An enormous amount of life is repetition. The seasons, day, and night come around again and again. Breathing, heartbeats, waking and sleeping, digestion and excretion, and other body rhythms are vital for survival, and they are all coded into the DNA whose reproduction is essential for any life at all. There are life cycles of birth, growth, aging, and death. Much of each day is routine: waking up, dressing, washing, eating and drinking, and so on. There are other patterns over longer periods—the week, the month, the year. The regularities of money can dictate a lot—when we get paid or when mortgage or tax or credit card payments are due, and lack of regularity can be disastrous. Through all this, there are our habits, from reading stories to our children or watching favorite television programs, through shopping, hobbies, and attending group meetings, to disciplines of physical exercise, keeping in touch with friends and family, visits to the pub, or prayer.

The importance of repetition is underlined by the number of inventions that assist us with it. My smart phone alone lets me record conversations, reproduce faces or events in photographs or video, photocopy a page, play music as often as I wish, play and replay games, resend or listen again to messages, and do much more than I have even learned. For many people, it has also replaced the most common machine on the planet, the watch or clock, which allows us to measure repeated units of time. The computer on which I am composing this book has numerous "re-" words among its commands: restart, repeat, replace, review, reveal, reject, redo, refresh, and more.

## Rereading

Repetition is especially fascinating and important in the sphere of meaning. The richer and deeper the meaning, the more we need to remember it, record it, retell it to ourselves and others, return to it from many angles, reflect on it, rethink it, re-search it. Think of crucial events in life, such as formative childhood experiences; getting to know a friend, husband, or wife; the birth of a child; the death of someone close; being successful or failing at an interview or other test; being betrayed or let down; or working on a project that went well. After much reflection and many retellings, they become even more meaningful, though sometimes we have to revise our understanding of them. In the drama of living, those retellings and revisions can be the key to making sense of our lives and opening a better future. As Micheal O'Siadhail says in "Duration":

> The constant edits, rewrites or redirection
> And yet to believe we haven't lost the plot

But keep on relearning and switching role
As if to follow a plot but not the plotting

As if forgivingly we go improvising on
A performance art still beyond control,

Duration's every knotting and unknotting
Gentling us towards whatever dénouement.[1]

How are we to *keep on relearning* and *forgivingly . . . go improvising on*? There are few things so fundamental as learning to reread as well as possible. Poetry itself might be understood as being written in order to be reread repeatedly. It can use rhythms, rhymes, and wordplay that help to make it memorizable—learning words by heart is perhaps the most effective and satisfying form of rereading. It is striking how many lines of the most widespread form of verse in our culture, popular songs, have been remembered by so many people. In addition to rhyme (the last six lines above are *a b c a b c*) and meter, a poem's imagery often has many possible meanings and connections whose density requires slow thinking and rethinking for them to emerge. The above quotation begins by evoking the process of writing and rewriting; the *or redirection* switches to—what? It can refer to the direction of travel on our journey of life, but the next line brings us into the world of drama. We may ask, is there a hint of a director or even an author of the play? This may be reinforced by mentioning *the plot*—or maybe not: it is only possible to *follow a plot but not the plotting*. The repeated *as if* makes sure we do not take it too literally and also stimulates imagining a range of possible meanings. We are in the midst of the messy unpredictability of "real life," requiring forgiveness for things in the past and risking *improvising on* into the future, yet recognizing that we are conditioned and constrained with so much *beyond control*.

Each of the three parts of "Duration" uses the image of the theater in seeking wisdom for life. In the light of the final couplet and its movement *towards whatever dénouement* (a French word used for the resolution of a play's plot, literally meaning "untying" or "unknotting"—this sailing imagery recurs throughout *Love Life*), we can reread the first part of the poem and find more meaning than on first reading:

> Open stage, no hiding wings,
> Mood swings, every scenario,
> Dreams, hurts, coups, failings,
> Space to let each other grow,
> Our repertoire of knockabout,
> Kitchen sink and passion play,
> To know our parts inside out,
> To choose rehearsed naïveté
> Of moments taken one by one.
> Often mothered in my wound,
> Sometimes do I daughter you?
> Subtle timings, shifts of cue,
> Day by day played in the round,
> Ad-lib an ease of layered duration.

This reminds us that the poem, and the whole of *Love Life*, is about the "extraordinary ordinary" of daily married life, *knockabout / Kitchen sink and passion play*. We play many roles with each other, timing can be vital, and so on. The mothering and daughtering, together with the *hurts*, *failings*, and *wounds* (and, in the unquoted middle part, the *gaffes*, *blunders*, *doubting*, and *let-downs*) all pour meaning into two key words in the last four lines: *forgivingly* and *gentling*. How we need to have our past reread and retold with compassionate forgiveness! And in the midst of all our worries, fears, and doubts, how we long to be "gentled" with word, look, and touch—I think of the L'Arche footwashing and other practices of *la tendresse* discussed in the previous chapter.

The exploration of just this poem could go on and on, rereading it in the light of the rest of *Love Life* and the rest of

O'Siadhail's poetry with which there are multiple resonances. We could go wider—there is also a reference to Shakespeare's *Hamlet* and a proverb-like saying from the great Irish playwright Brian Friel, *confusion is not an ignoble state*, which has vivid illustrations in his plays. To write about these few lines has led me to reread them twenty or more times, but that is not likely to be the end of it. I can return to these lines when prompted by new events or experiences, or when I am looking for something to write on a wedding anniversary card. And hopefully some readers will join in and find further resonances and be prompted to revise, rewrite, or redirect their lives to the accompaniment of rereading, relearning, forgiving, gentling, and *improvising on*.

Such practices affect our ways of habitually perceiving and thinking about our lives and those of others, enhance our sensitivity, shape our understanding and imagination, and deepen our wisdom. This *ripening* as *a knowing ferments in us* is a theme in "Orchard":

> First go around, it seemed enough to succumb
> To the telling, wonder how a plot would unfold,
> A one-way journey towards whatever outcome.
> But is a story richer the second time it's told,
> And beginnings subtler seen in the light of an end?
> A knowing ferments in us, a ripening enzyme,
> A looped story where the start and finish blend,
> Two-way traffic, a sort of doubling up of time.[2]

The *doubling up of time* echoes the title of the collection from which this is taken, *Our Double Time*. There, rereading plays a key role in the intensification and "doubling" of life, above all in the face of death. "Rehearsals"[3] explores it through savoring the major novel *Kristin Lavransdatter* by the Nobel Prize–winning Norwegian Sigrid Undset, through Sophocles's tragedy *Antigone* (which has inspired many other dramas and

81

stories) and through the Gospel of John's story (chapter 11) of the raising of Lazarus. But it is framed by a child's delight in *giddy piggyback rides*, tracing our passion for repetition back to some of our earliest pleasures.

Those giddy piggyback rides we called "broncos."
Giggling charges, feigned bucking and neighing.
I plead in half-light "O Father let's keep playing!"
"Alright," he said, "Then just three more gos."

Passion's careless caring for a man so carefree.
I travel the universe of Kristin Lavransdatter
As scene by scene her life worms into me
Making mine whatever time had taught her.
Somehow a story's contours shape my own.
All her desire, her grudges, her joy, her conviction.
Year in, year out it almost seems I've grown
Through her, as if I've been apprentice to a fiction.
I watch with her, struggling, lingering heroine,
As she takes off the wedding ring she entrusts
To her friend and glimpses a finger's scarred skin
Where love had made its mark beyond its lusts.
So silence and a piercing light. I was there.
Rehearsal and preview for one grand première.

Antigone's sisterhood, Creon's rigid city.
And Gods egging on that mix of choice and fate
As a chorus admonishes us in terror and pity:
"You've learned justice, although it comes too late."
Antigone distraught embraces her bridal tomb,
Stern Creon, a man so stunted in his growth.
"Any greatness in a human life brings doom,
Rigid citizen and sister." And am I both?
Heroine and hero. Part and counterpart
My Antigone hankers after perfect dreams,
In Creon I cry: "O crimes of my wicked heart!"
Antigone bereft. Antigone departed in her prime.
Like Lazarus, I return to live in double time.

Giddy up! Giddy up! I spur my bucking bronco,
Shoulder-high and giggling for all I'm worth.
Redoubled delight of only one more go.
My father lowering me gently back to earth.[4]

Note that the delight is not just in the repetition. The *only one more go*, and the unrepeatability of the last go, are about the even more important reality of uniqueness, singularity, the fact that we only live our lives once. Rereading the story of Kristin is a *rehearsal and preview for one grand première*—the one-off living of life that we cannot repeat. After entering into *Antigone* and identifying with both the heroine and King Creon who condemned her to death, *I return to live in double time*. It is that sense we sometimes have, when putting down a novel, or when the lights go on in a cinema or theater, or after switching off the television, that now we are ready to think and live differently, and better, because of what we have seen and heard.

### Religious Reading and the Gospel of John

Much religious practice is about such immersion, rereading, and rehearsal for the sake of richer, deeper, and more intense engagement in life. Explaining what religion is about is a little like trying to convey the experience of a favorite novel, film, poem, or piece of music. We may ourselves have come to appreciate it only slowly, after many years, or we may be gripped by different aspects of it now than when we first encountered it. It has helped to shape us, and we have changed our understanding of it as we have changed; for example, *Middlemarch* read at fifteen seems a different book to *Middlemarch* reread at fifty. Whole communities can have this experience, as the Jewish textual scholars and philosophers in the Textual Reasoning group did as they reread the Tanakh and Talmud together in the aftermath of the Shoah.[5] Even without such trauma, the literature, music, film, or drama that mean most to us are constantly yielding further meaning as we remember and rehearse them in the aftermath of fresh experience. So in inviting others to understand our religion, we actually want them to have at least a taste of the sort of abundant meaning that can only be had by practices that involve a great deal of repetition in order to go deeper and inspire living differently. One of the reasons Scriptural Reasoning, as described in chapter 2, works for so many people is that it allows participants in one tradition of rereading to share a little in other traditions of rereading.

In the preface to his remarkable study, *Religious Reading: The Place of Reading in the Practice of Religion*, Paul Griffiths says,

> So far as I can recall, I have always been able to read, to make sense of and be excited by written things. I know, of course, that there was a time when I could not read; it's just that I cannot remember it. But I was never taught, and have still not properly learned, how to read with careful, slow attentiveness; it is difficult for me to read with the goal of incorporating what I read, of writing it upon the pages of my memory; I find it hard to read as a lover, to caress, lick, smell, and savor the words on the page, and to return to them ever and again. I read, instead, mostly as a consumer, someone who wants to extract what is useful or exciting or entertaining from what is read, preferably with dispatch, and then move on to something else. . . . I'm not alone in this condition. Most academic readers are consumerist in their reading habits, and this is because they, like me, have been taught to be so and rewarded for being so. But I've also spent a good portion of my life trying to understand what it means to be a Christian, as well as much time studying literary works composed by Indian Buddhists. Both of these practices have gradually led me to see that consumerist reading isn't the only kind there is. It's also possible to read religiously, as a lover reads, with a tensile attentiveness that wishes to linger, to prolong, to savor, and has no interest at all in the quick orgasm of

consumption. Reading religiously, I've come to think, is central to being religious. Losing, or never having, the ability so to read is tantamount to losing, or never having, the ability to offer a religious account of things.[6]

It is not only academic readers who are consumerist. It is worth asking ourselves how much of our reading is consumerist in Griffiths's sense and how much time we spend in "religious reading" as he describes it, whether of religious or other texts.

Our electronic technologies of reproduction might seem biased toward consumerist reading. They give access to vast quantities of material to be read, and there is pressure to keep up-to-date, whether with emails, text messages, memos, websites of professional or personal interest, Facebook, tweets, the news, or the multitude of attachments and downloads.

Yet, on the other hand, the sheer volume makes it understandable if we do not keep up, so the pressure of expectation can be eased, and increasing numbers of people are developing personal disciplines, often aided by software, that enable them to concentrate on the more urgent and important, and to prioritize responses. Electronic access and searches can save a great deal of time that used to send us to libraries or archives or make us leaf through books and journals. Above all, most of the great classic texts have online resources, some superb, that enable us to expand and deepen our understanding. Hypertext lets us click on a word or verse and find out how it has been translated and the range of meanings that have been proposed for it over the centuries and around the world today. Once we find a commentator or interpreter who is really good, we can quickly find out what else they have written and often access it at once. We can become part of an online community (which can be very select) of those we respect and trust as interpreters. All of this can complement face-to-face reading with others: the richness of the face-to-face can be accompanied between meetings by the reach and convenience of email, a chat room, or Skype.

So, as with many inventions that can enhance life (I think of car or air travel, nuclear energy, banks, marriage), electronic communication can also do damage, cause complications, go wrong, or be a curse. But, as with writing and reading (which once were new inventions, often suspect, and only slowly became central to religions, cultures, and civilizations), on balance most of us would prefer to have them than not. The challenge is how to sustain and even enhance religious reading as part of a drama of living in which electronic communication plays a role.

The Gospel of John was written by a religious reader for religious readers to encourage rereaders and draw them further along **"the way,"** deeper into **"the truth,"** and more fully into **"life"** (John 14:6). John teaches how to read his Gospel by showing how he himself reads his Scriptures, and he writes so as to attract us to inhabit his words, indwelling and abiding in them by continual rereading. How does he do this?

The very first words of his Gospel repeat the opening words of his Bible: **In the beginning . . .** (Gen. 1:1—Septuagint *en archē*; John 1:1—*en archē*). Especially in his opening chapters and closing chapters, there are many resonances with the opening chapters of Genesis—for example, just in his first chapter and in Genesis 1, we find God, life, light, darkness, world, spirit, day, called, came into being/became, water, heaven, seeing, and more. John was clearly steeped in the Septuagint through constant rereading, and his writing reflects this. He quotes less from the Septuagint than the other Gospels do but makes more indirect allusions to it. What scholars call "intertextuality"—one text resonating with another—runs all through John. His Prologue alone echoes not only Genesis but also the rest of the Torah, several wisdom writings (including the passage from the Wisdom of Solomon quoted in chapter 2 above), and the prophets of Israel. It is always worthwhile rereading John alongside the texts he alludes to—this helps to illuminate both. And just as he himself is immersed in his Scriptures as a religious reader, so he invites us to be immersed in both them and the text he writes.

It is also always worth reading the other Gospels alongside John. Scholars differ in their opinions about how much of the Synoptic Gospels or the traditions behind them John had read or received orally. I am becoming more and more convinced that John knew at least Mark and Luke, and that he has internalized earlier Christian tradition through immersion in their writing and in eyewitness testimony. His reception of all this encourages us to inhabit the Synoptics as well as the Septuagint, allowing them, too, to illuminate John as he illuminates them.

A third "intertext" for John is his own Gospel (scholars call this "intratextuality"). It is carefully crafted with all sorts of themes and cross-references within it. The more one rereads him the more internal resonances emerge—and he writes in such a way as to inspire the reader to find these even where he himself may not have intended them. It is as if he sets an example of creative rereading of the Septuagint and the Synoptics and then expects readers to do something similar for themselves, not only with those texts but also with his own.

When, for example, O'Siadhail writes of *beginnings subtler seen in the light of an end*, that is certainly so in John. After reading the whole Gospel, one returns to elements of the prologue with new eyes. Most embracing and fundamental of all, God is understood differently after the drama has culminated in Thomas's address to the risen Jesus: **"My Lord and my God!"** (John 20:28). "Word," "life," "light," "darkness," "sending," "testimony," "believing," "knowing," "name," "birth," and other terms have all gathered fresh meaning, redefined through one scene of the drama after another. Perhaps most striking has been the transformation of "flesh" (*sarx*) and "glory" (*doxa*).

The prologue says of Jesus: **And the Word became flesh and lived among us, and we have seen his glory, the glory as of a father's only son, full of grace and truth** (1:14). As the Gospel goes on, both flesh and glory are given new content by what happens in the drama, climaxing in Jesus's death. John daringly calls the crucifixion Jesus's glorification. The mortal, vulnerable flesh of Jesus is the place where God's glory is reconceived as love that gives its life for others. There is no mention of love or of the death of Jesus in the prologue, but by the end of the story these have filled out the meaning of its key terms, such as "flesh" and "glory," which we understand differently on rereading.

The ending returns to its beginnings with retrospective illumination in other ways too. I think that John even goes back to the opening words of Genesis 1:1. In the Greek, that reads *en archē epoiēsen ho theos* . . . (**In the beginning God created/ made/did . . .**). John opens his Gospel with *en archē* . . . (**In the beginning . . .**), and at the end of both chapter 20 and chapter 21, he has *epoiēsen ho Iēsous* (**Jesus did/made/created**—20:30; 21:25). It is as if the whole Gospel has been bracketed by the opening words of Genesis, slipped in between the *en archē* and the *epoiésen*, but by the end of the Gospel, the God of Genesis has been identified fully with Jesus.

Besides his own text and those of the Synoptic Gospels and the Old Testament/Septuagint, John's Gospel can fruitfully be read alongside many other texts and can be rethought in engagement with any rich concentration of meaning. He sets the context for interpretation by saying that **all things came into being** through the Word, whose **life was the light of all people** (1:3–4). So the meaning of his Gospel cries out to be connected with all reality, including all peoples, religions, cultures, arts, sciences, and ordinary lives. In the early centuries of Christianity, John's vision of Jesus connecting with **all things** stimulated wide-ranging and complex engagement with the sophisticated civilization in which the church developed. Now the stimulus is global, as this text is read and reread in every country of the world.

So each new intertext and context stimulates rereading. So also does John's way of writing. How can you ever come to the end of meditating on the meaning of his core symbols such as light and darkness, bread, water, wine and vine, wind, and many more, especially when they also have resonances in the rest of the Bible and across cultures, religions, and civilizations? Many of his apparently ordinary words accumulate layer after layer of meaning as his story unfolds. One example is the Greek verb just mentioned, *poiein*, meaning "do," "make," or "create"; another is *menein*, meaning "continue," "remain," "stay," or "abide," which was discussed above in chapter 1. He often communicates his meaning in waves—the first goes up so far then ceases, to be followed by another that covers the same ground but goes a little further. The last wave is usually the one to watch especially: it reaches the key point.

An example is the story of Nicodemus in 3:1–21. The first, short wave ends in verse 3 with Jesus saying, **"Very truly, I tell you, no one can see the kingdom of God without being born from above"** (or **born again**—the Greek can mean either; here, as often, John makes sure we reread and rethink by using a word with more than one meaning). The second wave extends the birth image to being **"born of water and Spirit"** (or **wind**—the Greek again has two meanings, which John plays on: **"The wind/spirit blows where it chooses"** [v. 8]). Then comes the final long wave, from verse 12 to verse 21. This is extraordinarily dense. It reaches back to themes of John 1 (testimony, believing, Son of Man, Moses, the world, the Son of God, light, and darkness) and adds to them others that are crucial in the rest of the Gospel: the crucifixion of Jesus (described as him being **lifted up**), eternal life, judgment, and God's love for the world. This last wave has both gone over ground covered earlier and taken us further. It is nonidentical repetition, repetition with variation, a theme with improvisation; these are essential in a drama with both continuity and innovation.

The very end of that passage has a striking little phrase about deeds **"done in God"** (v. 21). John makes it very clear that he does not just want readers or even rereaders: he wants readers who act, who reread in order to act better, and who, above all, love. He speaks of **"those who do what is true"** (v. 21): the truth in this Gospel is primarily to be done, and what is to be done is, supremely, to love. It is an intensely activist Gospel, as seen in the leading role of dramatic narrative. It wants readers to encounter Jesus and therefore mostly describes encounters of Jesus. It also wants readers to be inspired to do even greater things. But this is the activism of love and therefore springs from the heart of a relationship. Hence the **done in God**. That little word **"in"** might be used as a key to John's whole theology, as expressed in the simplicity and inexhaustible depth of Jesus's final prayer at his last supper: **"I in them and you in me, that they may become completely one . . . so that the love with which you have loved me may be in them, and I in them"** (John 17:23, 26). Rereading too can be done in love, in faith and trust, in community—embraced by that capacious **"in"** and oriented to a life of loving.

## Rehearsing for Life

Preparation, which might be seen as "repetition in advance," is obviously a vital part of life. Without it, we not only do worse at an examination, an interview, a speech, a musical performance, a court appearance, or some other "set piece" task; it is also essential for handling any difficult or complex situation and above all for coping with relationships. Think of all those hours spent rehearsing what to say, what to do, and how to respond in relationships with parents, lovers, children, friends, colleagues, or enemies. It is the time spent before a sensitive meeting, or before picking up the phone, or while agonizing over the right phrasing for a memo, letter, email, or tweet.

In any major group activity, preparation needs to be well thought through and organized. In drama, which I have been taking as one of the main ways to think about life in these chapters, it involves rehearsal, taking far more time than the onstage performance. I remember sitting in a church hall in London watching the Royal Shakespeare Company rehearsing Ibsen's *Brand* with Ralph Fiennes in the title role. What lasted a few minutes when it was performed on stage took up the whole rehearsal. It was a ghost scene, and every movement, expression, implication, and nuance of possible meaning was explored. There were discussions and some differences between director and actors; at one point they referred back to the Norwegian original, and moves and lines were repeated time and time again.

Likewise, most of military life is spent not fighting but preparing to fight. The ninety minutes of a football match requires many hours of exercise, practice, and discussion of tactics, backed by years of experience. Most food is eaten more quickly than it is prepared: even "instant" meals take someone's time—in growing, precooking, packaging, delivering, and retailing. The birthday party, the business initiative, the political campaign, the radio or television program, the holiday, and so on; a large part of the secret of success is the quality of preparation before the event. Any worthwhile job or profession requires thorough preparation, often years of it.

A great deal of religion can be seen as preparation for life as a whole. It is made up of habits and practices that are meant to shape our days, weeks, and years by drawing on wisdom that has accumulated over centuries and is constantly being rethought, reapplied, and improvised on. All of us are shaped by habits and forms of preparation in the main areas of our lives. Key questions are: How wise are they? Do they draw on good sources of wisdom and experience? Do they give us a well-balanced "ecology" of life, not only in face-to-face relations with others but also in our habits of body, heart, mind, and imagination, all set within a big picture of the meaning and purpose of living?

Those are not questions that can be answered satisfactorily in a "consumerist" way, by looking at what is available, trying various products, and then deciding which is the best on the market. Our culture does, of course, have much consumer "pick and mix" religion, and many of us understandably go through a period of experimentation, often with a good deal of confusion or indecision. But genuinely life-shaping habits and practices are by definition long-term and require at some point a long-term commitment.

### Rehearsing for the Day

A life-shaping moment for me during my student years was when a wise Anglican monk told me for the first time about what he called "the daily office." I had not heard of it before under that name. He explained that it is a pattern of daily Bible reading, worship of God, and prayer for others and oneself, and that it need not take more than fifteen minutes. It has Jewish roots thousands of years old, has been developed in various forms by Christians, and there are now several well–worked-out patterns in different Christian traditions. He recommended one that was a pilot for the pattern in the Church of England's *Common Worship*, which I now use. After explaining it, he said, "Try it for five or ten years and see if it works."

I did, and it has worked. It has accompanied me day in, day out (though, of course, with some days missed for good or bad reasons) decade after decade. It is like the DNA of my day.

It is my "code" for living that taps into ancient wisdom that has been constantly renewed century after century and can be improvised on afresh today. It sets me within a whole ecosystem of meaning and practice. It connects me with God above all, with other worshipers in the past and present, with the people God loves (all, without exception) and the creation God loves, and with past, present, and future acts in the drama of God's involvement with the world. It is the horizon for the day (which otherwise might only be given by the morning news or my personal concerns), and a rehearsal for the day. To pray for people and tasks in the day ahead is a form of preparation that can—usually slowly, but occasionally with flashes of inspiration or surges of love and forgiveness—transform our ways of engaging with them. And, time permitting, the pattern allows for many variations—silent meditation, singing or chanting, rumination on a biblical passage, reading from another book, wrestling with some difficult or anguished matter before God, or simply heart-to-heart conversation in prayer—the face-to-unseen-face of faith and love.

One of the benefits of electronic communication is that what is needed—the pattern of the "daily office," the "lectionary" (a list of short readings from the Bible set for each day of the year) and even the Bible itself—is all available online or in apps for a smart phone, though I still prefer well-worn books and lists on paper of the people, groups, and issues that call for regular prayer.

### Rehearsing for the Week and for the Sabbath

Every so often, it is possible physically to share in the daily office with others, rather than just doing it alone while knowing that I am in communion with tens of millions of others who are following this or some other daily pattern of worship, Bible reading, and prayer. Some do have joint daily prayer as a regular part of life, but probably most Christians gather with others for worship once a week at best. The pattern is, again, deeply Jewish, rooted in the Genesis creation story and God's rest on the seventh day, the Sabbath: **And on the seventh day God finished the work that he had done, and he rested on the seventh day from all the work that he had done. So God blessed the seventh day and hallowed it, because on it God rested from all the work that he had done in creation** (Gen. 2:2–3).

The wisdom of the Sabbath has a great deal in common with that of the daily office or of any good habit: taste and see! Keep the Sabbath for some years and notice the difference. In the book to which the present one is a sequel, *The Shape of Living*, I quoted a rabbi who was asked in a television interview, "How have the Jews managed to preserve the Sabbath over thousands of years?" His reply was, "It is not the Jews who have preserved the Sabbath. The Sabbath has preserved the Jews."[7]

As often with wisdom, many elements come together in the Sabbath. There is rest as not working. Work, and the urgency of getting things done, is one of the most powerful compulsions in our civilization. For many, it is an addiction, and as soon as one thing is finished another immediately presses to be done. A day when work and its compulsions are interrupted can seem like a waste of time. The notion that to stop working can be as healthy a discipline as to work simply appears odd. All sorts of economic, social, psychological, and domestic pressures can conspire against taking a break from work, especially for a whole day and night (or, for Jews who begin *Shabbat* at sundown, a night and day). Yet the wisdom of this break goes far beyond helping those obsessed with work. Our culture is filled with other compulsions and addictions, some but not all related to work: to have money and possessions; to be successful; to have power, influence, recognition and status; to be fit, beautiful, and attractive. To keep the Sabbath is a sign of hope that they need not dominate us, since the daily continuity of their grip is broken for at least a while.

But rest is more than not working. It is a positive thing in itself, and the rich Jewish wisdom of the Sabbath includes a celebratory meal with prayer and singing, family time, hospitality, lovemaking, study of Torah, conversation, walking, not making others work, rest for farm animals, and much else. A day off work can stimulate creativity in face-to-face relations, in the time one has to oneself, and in the way one appreciates the natural world. The only really effective antidotes to bad habits are good habits. Keeping the Sabbath wisely and creatively is a good compulsion or addiction, though, as in other spheres, here too the corruption of the best is the worst, and the Sabbath has often been kept unwisely or made into an instrument of oppression. At its best, it is a form of repetition week-by-week that opens up a time for remembering, restoration, and fresh improvisation.

It can also give us a different perspective on the rest of the week, both the one that has just ended and the one to come. Jews keep the Sabbath on Saturday, the last day of the week; most Christians keep it on Sunday, the first day (though in the way many diaries are printed Sunday now is the last day). There is wisdom in both—rest after the week's work, or before it. But the experienced reality for both Jews and Christians is "both/ and"; this day is not simply one in a sequence, it is both an ending and a beginning, a special time of its own that has the capacity to embrace and be a blessing for all other time. In its light, we may reappraise the value of work done and planned. But even that is too instrumental, too work oriented, too sequential. The Sabbath's blessing is not just to help us flourish the rest of the week. It is a joy in itself. It has freedom *from* work and *from* other daily concerns for the sake of freedom *for* enjoyment of each other, food, sex, study, exercise, play, the natural world—and God.

The Sabbath can be seen as rehearsal for the rest of the week, preparing for the days to come through being "wise in the Spirit," resourcing our bodies, minds, spirits, and face-to-face. But it goes beyond rehearsal and preparation; the Sabbath itself is a weekly event in the one-off drama of living. It might be truer to see the other six days as a rehearsal for the Sabbath.

The wisdom of the Sabbath spreads out in many directions. Once one is in the habit of keeping the Sabbath, it can help to generate other habits—or the other habits can cultivate a desire for the Sabbath. There can be little Sabbaths in the day—times when we pause, rest, delight in something or someone, recollect in quiet, savor a sight or sound or taste or touch or scent, or read "religiously" as Paul Griffiths describes it. There can be longer Sabbaths in the year or over many years—festivals, holidays, pilgrimages, retreats, courses of study, or learning an art or craft or sport done just for the delight of it, and other things that creatively break into our routines and continuities. The Bible applies the sabbatical principle to the land (resting it every seventh year, restoring it to its original owner after forty-nine years) and to debt (forgiving it every seven years), and in a world threatened by environmental catastrophe and oppressed by massive debt, both national and personal, this is now being taken more seriously.

The Jewish greeting *shabbat shalom*, "Sabbath peace," suggests the scope. *Shalom* is not just "peace" as the absence of war or conflict but the full flourishing of human beings and the whole of creation. God is the God of peace:

> The LORD spoke to Moses, saying: Speak to Aaron and his sons, saying, Thus you shall bless the Israelites: You shall say to them,
>> The LORD bless you and keep you;
>>> the LORD make his face to shine upon you, and be gracious to you;

96

the LORD lift up his countenance upon you, and give
you peace.
So they shall put my name on the Israelites, and I will bless
them. (Num. 6:22–27)

In the Genesis story God blesses the Sabbath; in Numbers
the pattern of the priestly blessing culminates in the gift of
shalom. The Sabbath is a weekly renewal of God's blessing, and
it is inseparable from being before the face of the unseen God,
receiving peace, bearing **"my name."** The practical conclusion
is obvious, and it has been drawn by both Jews and Christians
and practiced century after century: God is to be worshiped
on the Sabbath, and God's name, who God is, is to be blessed,
honored, hallowed, glorified, sanctified, praised, rejoiced in.

There are many good reasons (as well as many bad ones)
to take part in weekly worship of God as Christians. It is a response to numerous biblical instructions to love God, remember
God, praise God, thank God, sing to God, ask of God, repent
to God, and **"Do this in remembrance of me"** (Luke 22:19).
Worship bonds us as a community; we can do all those things
together, listening to the Bible and to teaching, repenting, and
being forgiven; uniting in prayer for ourselves and the world;
talking to each other; welcoming others into the community;
and being inspired to go out to serve others and take part collab-
oratively as a community in the drama of living. Good worship
is multifaceted, and it can draw us closer to one another and to
God through hearing, speaking and music, beauty, taste, scent,
movement, and shared feeling. Because we are people of habit
who are formed through repetition, reciting, rereading, and rehearsing, we are foolish if we do not build those practices into
our life week by week. What could be a better use of our time?

But through all and above all it is about God. The fundamental reason for taking part is that we do it for God's sake. To be
before God in worship is not only rehearsal for the rest of life;

this is living life to the full, gathering it up before the One who creates and energizes it—living in the awesome presence of God.

## Beyond Rehearsal: Classic Surprises

Rehearsal, then, is a helpful idea for the vital dimension of preparation, repetition, and practice in life, but it has its limitation built into it: the main point of rehearsal is live dramatic performance. O'Siadhail's rereading of *Kristin Lavransdatter* and *Antigone* led to him returning to *live in double time*. Rereading John, praying the daily office, or worshiping weekly in church can be profoundly formative of who we are and how we think, imagine, and act in the rest of our lives, but they are also events in the drama in their own right. All the repetition, practice, and rehearsal cannot prepare us for what might happen as we take seriously the fact that, in studying John, opening our day in prayer, listening to a sermon, or taking part in the Eucharist, we are actually in the presence of a God of surprises.

There can be a healthy skepticism, even radical suspicion, of religious practices that seem to claim that they give access to God. It is God who gives access to God. We simply desire and ask. Indeed, even our desiring and asking are enabled by God. Our practices can be seen as continual desiring and asking. In God's presence, we are being desired far more passionately than we ever desire. We are "being read" more perceptively than we can ever read. We are questioned more radically than we ever question. We are being searched for more thoroughly than we search. We are being spoken to, listened to, affirmed, and taught. We are being invited into a wisdom and a love that we have hardly begun to desire wholeheartedly. We are blessed before and as we bless.

As that fundamental receptivity toward God is opened up within us, both individually and in groups and communities, surprises happen again and again. Some of these are unique events with no close parallels. But there are also what one might call classic surprises. They keep on happening in certain settings to which we repeatedly return, or in association with certain practices or people. Despite something like it happening many times before, each time it happens it is fresh and new. In ordinary life, one thinks of the smile or laughter of a child, dear friend, or lover; seeing again one of the great plays of Shakespeare; or a garden in springtime. What about the Christian life of faith? Each person and community will have their own favorite testimonies. I conclude this chapter by mentioning just three that are associated with some of the practices discussed in this chapter.

### The Daily Office and Praying the Collects

In several Christian traditions, including my own Anglican one, there is a set prayer called a "collect" for every week of the Christian year and for festivals and other special occasions. Some of them go back to much earlier liturgies, having survived many processes of selection, and others are more recent. They are short, carefully crafted, and dense with biblical content. Taken together, the collects give a balanced, nourishing diet for Christian faith and practice. In the mode of prayer, they move through the Christian year, covering the main events of the Christian drama from creation to consummation and paying special attention to the birth, baptism, transfiguration, death, resurrection, and ascension of Jesus, followed by the giving of the Holy Spirit at Pentecost and the life of discipleship in the church. They often combine core teaching with Christian practice. If one were to meditate on each of these, allowing it to form one's mind and imagination and orient one's prayer, reading, and action, the result would be a life shaped by the biblical drama and resourced by theology distilled from centuries of Christian experience and wisdom.

The surprise for me has been what many others have also found: how extraordinarily fruitful the collects are year after year. Repeated use allows more and more meaning to pour into them and fuller engagement with God to come through them. Of course, I believed those who have said this before me, but one mark of a classic surprise is that this sort of testimony does not communicate much. It is like talking about a taste before it is on the palate. The tasting happens through the year with a different seasonal collect to be savored each week.

## Rereading and Reconciliation

Scriptural Reasoning, in which Jews, Christians, and Muslims (and increasingly other traditions too) gather in conversation around their Scriptures, has been described above in chapter 2 as a wisdom-seeking practice of dramatic dialogue across differences. This chapter has suggested that part of its attraction lies in bringing three or more traditions of rereading together. The classic surprises that come to Christians—for example, through rereading the Gospel of John—have their analogies in Jewish and Muslim rereadings of their classic texts. To bring together the disciplines and delights of rereading in the three traditions not only multiplies the surprises but also enables and to some extent realizes a distinctive form of reconciliation between religions that have long histories of division and conflict and are still often deeply and dangerously alienated from each other.

As I look at a range of small-scale Scriptural Reasoning initiatives in the UK, US, Canada, Ireland, continental Europe, Russia, China, and the Middle East, I see a capacity (still in its very early days) for bringing about long-term reconciliation that is related to the practice of "religious reading." Wrestling with deep and often difficult texts to which one can return again and again without exhausting their meaning helps create long-term collegiality and often friendship. Learning of other traditions, beliefs, and practices from the inside, through face-to-face sharing, can give a quality of understanding that not only allows for recognizing similarities and agreements but also for improving the quality of irresolvable disagreement about dissimilarities, divisions, and conflicts. And, because deep division usually has complex historical roots, with conflicting versions of them retold by each side, any hope of more than superficial engagement requires the disciplines of patient rereading, retelling, reinterpreting, and rethinking in the presence of each other. They can even create at least some of the conditions for repentance, reconciliation, and renewal.

## *Worship and "At Night a Song Is with Me"*

In 2011, the composer Rob Mathes conducted two soloists, two choirs, an orchestra, and a rhythm section in the world premiere of "At Night a Song Is with Me" in Greenwich, Connecticut. The lyrics were a combination of Psalms from the Bible and responses to them in songs by O'Siadhail, and the music by Mathes was a blend of classical, jazz, and other genres. The Psalms are perhaps the most repeated part of the Bible, being central to both Jewish and Christian worship for millennia. Here they were being sung to new music and answered by new songs, giving yet another classic surprise.

Between Psalm 121, **I lift up my eyes to the hills**, and Psalm 139, **O LORD, you have searched me and known me**, O'Siadhail's responsive song, "Hand," reaches for the double richness of relearning and the superabundance of more and more to be discovered, all in the context of a vast cosmos and the mystery of God.

> You only know, you never know—
> The more you know, the more you'll find
> A world above, a world below
> A hand lays out beyond your mind
>
> What you once learned you learn once more—
> You bit the apple, bite the peach—

101

The sky you'd thought you could explore
A hand has slung beyond your reach.

Go count the galaxies by night
Be glad the mind can reach so far,
Go count the billion years of light
A hand has stretched beyond your star.

You only know, you never know—
The more you know, the more you'll find
A world above, a world below
A hand lays out beyond your mind.[8]

Soon after this came "FINALE—SING!!!! (Psalm 148)," whose choral, orchestral, and solo crescendo had the whole audience standing and clapping in climactic repetition:

All his angels, all his hosts,
Sun and moon and shining stars,
Young and old together, sing!

From the earth and from all deeps,
Fire and hail and snow and frost,
Young and old together, sing!

For his glory, for his name
Men and women, sing!

Stormy winds and mountains,
Every hill and every stream,
Young and old together, sing!

Living things on land and sea,
Flying birds and creeping things,
Young and old together, sing!

For his glory, for his name
Men and women, sing!

Glory, glory, glory, glory, glory, glory,
Sing! Sing!

# 5

# Loving

*Intimate, Dramatic, Ultimate*

For most of us, love is what matters most. Love may shape our lives in the labors and joys of mothering or fathering, of being a husband, wife, partner, son, daughter, lover, friend, follower, collaborator, team player, party member, patriot, or worshiper. But we are also shaped through the failure or partial failure of love—love denied, betrayed, distorted, perverted, trivialized, disappointed, embittered, unfulfilled, lost. Perhaps here above all the corruption of the best is the worst. The family is where most violence in our world happens, and many of the other generators of conflict and enmity also have a strong element of love—but love that has gone wrong: love of kin, tribe, land and nation, money, language, truth, justice, freedom, or religion. We tend to be most vulnerable and most violent (whether physically or in other ways, and whether turned against others or ourselves) in relation to our loves. But all this is testimony, both positive and negative, to love mattering most.

The earlier chapters lead directly to this one: lives as dramas of loving; the love of wisdom and the wisdom of love; the face-to-face as the primary perspective of love; and the essential role in long-term love of repetition, habit, remembering, retelling, rehearsal, reconsidering, repentance, repair, and renewal.

## Friendship

Friendship is perhaps the most varied and pervasive of loves. It is least bound into communities and institutions, and there is a freedom and chosenness about it that is often lacking in relationships of blood, work, locality, and religion. Yet it can also enter into and sometimes transform those relationships and even whole institutions or movements. It may be casual or a matter of life and death, and it may be one-to-one or one among many. Its demands on time can vary greatly. Friendship's endless surprises include the crossing of deep divisions, alienations, and even enmities. The world's civilizations and cultures are full of the wisdom of friendship and stories of friends.

It is easier to think of typical marriages or families than typical friendships, so the particular story of each is all the more important, and how its drama might develop is far less predictable. To say someone is my friend may mean practically nothing or almost everything. Micheal O'Siadhail in a poem written in his mid-thirties, "For My Friends," expresses this variation as part of a movement from more casual friendships in youth to *the precious weave* of lives becoming *interwoven*, sharing conflicts, burdens, and joys in the ups and downs of life, creating *the fabric of a common story*:

> Spendthrift friendships once ravelled and unravelled,
> Carefree leisurely as a journey without a plan;
> Easy-come, easy-go, there was a while I travelled

Lightly, made my friends catch-as-catch-can.
Gradually, the casual twisted the precious weave,
This tissue of feeling in which I have grown;
Though I follow a single thread, I must believe
That bound to the whole we never drift alone.
Crossed, matted fibres long inwrought,
Friendships prove the fabric of a common story,
The web which takes the strain of every thought,
Shares the fray or stain, joys in our glory.
Interwoven, at last I dare to move without misgiving;
I touch the invisible, love this gauze of living.[1]

The dedication in *Our Double Time*, published after O'Siadhail turned fifty, is, *For those voices within, my love and thanks.* The book wrestles with love and death (on the latter there will be more in the next chapter), and the final section, called "Voices," has a series of poems on friendship and particular friends. The image of interweaving is still there, but now it is taken up into the texture of language and of *knitted music*, especially the improvisation of jazz and the interplay of melodies in polyphony. "Overflow," the overture of the section, meditates on the voices of friends and how they fill our hearts:

The jazzmen say to improvise is both to hear
And answer at one time. Careless and austere,
How a knitted music revels in its discipline.
Friends and lovers, discrete polyphony within,
Where voices intersect, resonant and polyglot,
Do all our conversations tangle in one plot?
. . .
Line and texture of those voices in one heart . . .

Then in the central stanza, the sheer physicality of the voices of our "community of the heart" is savored as a medium of love, leading into the extraordinary logic of gratitude—the more

105

complete and delightful an experience or event, the more it cries out to go on being completed and delighted in through appreciation, thanks, and praise. It is all appropriately in rhyming couplets:

> Nothing woos like voices. Those breaths haul
> Ribs and midriff like a bucket handle. Of all
> Kisses this wells deepest. Diaphragm-dance.
> Air pumped to the head's cavities of resonance.
> Windpipe. Soundbox purr. A throat's hum.
> Tongue-shaped waves tap against an eardrum,
> . . .
> Every sound makes love. My body sings
> And sways to a tune. Sap leaps and rejoices,
> Juiced and warmed in this lavishness of voices.
> All praise my lovers, and listen how I grow,
> My voice welling in your voices' overflow.
> Completing a completion, abundance overspilt;
> As if I keep on filling what's already fulfilled.

The culminating stanza adds images of dancing and feasting to celebrate these voices that shape our life stories:

> O voices within shaping everything I do,
> Even in my soliloquies I collogue with you.
> Always, everywhere, ballet of voices in me.
> . . .
> A banquet of voices within steadying me
> When night's angel croons her minor key.
> Every leap, every turn our histories take
> Will have been a music we lived to make.[2]

The first friend he addresses, in "Matins for You," is his wife, Bríd. It is my favorite of all love poems, the more so for being a friendship poem too. Bríd is also daughter, schoolteacher,

enabler of the dreams of others, improviser, and mystery—
*Mistress Zen*:

Come again glistening from your morning shower
Half-coquettishly you'll throw
Your robe at me calling out "Hello! Hello!"
I turn over stretching out to snatch
A bundle from the air and once more to watch
That parade across your bower.
Jaunty, brisk, allegro,
Preparing improvisations of yet another day
As on our first morning twenty-seven years ago.

Sit on the bed-end and pull a stocking on,
Slip that frock over your head
Let it slither a little, ride your hips, then spread
Its folds and tumbles, flopping past those thighs
To swish against your ankles. I'm still all eyes.
The thrill and first frisson
At the half-known but unsaid,
At hints and contours embodied in a dance of dress
I'm ogling snugly from this your still warm bed.

Now you're hurrying, business-like and ready to go.
I wonder if I've ever glimpsed you
Or if all those years I even as much as knew
Behind those hints and suggestions I admire
What inmost aim or dream or heart's desire
Calls out "Hello, Hello!"
Flirt and peekaboo
Of such unwitting closeness, our take-for-grantedness,
Complex web of intimacies where we slowly grew.

Sometimes wells of aloneness seem almost to imbue
Your silence with the long wistful rubato
Of a Chopin nocturne or is it a seannós tremolo?
"Má bhíonn tú liom bí liom, gach orlach de do chroí

If you're mine be mine, each inch of your heart for me"
That infinite longing in you
A girl racing to follow
The bus's headlamps to meet your father at Bunbeg.
He steps down from the platform. Hello! Hello!

You smile your father's inward Zen-like smile.
And yet its light shines outward
As when I watched you helping a child to word
The coy, swaggering pleasure of new shoes,
A muse the more a muse in being a muse.
That inward outward smile
Delights in delight conferred,
Fine-tuning those strains and riffs of wishes unspoken,
Desires another's heart doesn't yet know it has heard.

Now I see you, now I don't. The doubt
And loneness of what's always new,
Moments seized in double time, love's impromptu,
As when late last night you started telling me
How even as a girl you'd known your dream would be
Bringing others' dreams about.
This once I think I glimpsed you,
You my glistening, lonely, giving Mistress Zen.
Thank you. Thank you for so many dreams come true.[3]

Then comes a series of poems for other friends and about friendship. Together, they distill a wisdom of friendship.

Between St. Francis and St. Clare are *faithful secrets*, so much left unsaid; the nurturing of each other's vocations—*each with our own, a life, a call*; keeping faith with each other year after year—*long-standing, long-headed, long-range patience*; and the deepening as each is true to his or her vocation—*a love thickening the more that love obeys*.[4]

In "Northway" there is

. . . her listening;
Gentle, anxious, keen, generous, intense,
All that giving and gift of utter presence. . . .
That poise of her attentiveness, the passionate answer.[5]

In "Oak" there are years of *side-by-sideness*; planning life journeys; playing various roles in each other's lives—father, brother, and more; *ramifying joy*; facing the unexpected together; *stretching to understand / To desire according to the desire of another*; sharing

> Dreams, tasks, troubles, secrets we confide,
> Double openness of growing side by side.

It all pivots around the risk of mutual, unconditional commitment:

> Our daring to say "Love me as I love you."[6]

In "Widening" there is the surprise possibility of a new friendship:

> I'm caught off guard by "love's sudden show."[7]

(The quotation is from Dante about Beatrice, translating the Italian *amor subitamente*.) Should I open up *the tighter circle of my friends*?

> Here at the core, will I dare to trust this inclusion?

This is one of the greatest mysteries of love: we do not just have a fixed amount of it. When our second child was born, she did not take away love from the first, nor did the third from the first two. Mysteriously, the heart seems to expand to embrace each new child, each new friend. Indeed, one of the great delights in life is to find a new friend through being introduced by an old friend. There are, of course, many factors to be taken into

109

account in having another child or beginning a new friendship. But if it seems right (or even if, in the case of a child, we have one without planning), we do not need to worry about the heart's capacity. "Widening" describes a friendship beginning later in life with that strange sense of recognition and "ringing true" one can have, as suddenly there is a new yet somehow familiar person among one's friends:

> That over the unknown, all the unshared heritage,
> Over so many missing years,
> *Amor subitamente* throws its invisible bridge.
>
> Yet more a return, like something meant to be.
> The best robe, the fatted calf.
> This feast is doubling its double time in me.
>
> Overwhelmed. Almost as if there's no choice,
> A circle gapes and opens its embrace.
> Hail and welcome! my new and prodigal voice.[8]

The last words of the "Voices" section (and of the collection) might also be the last (though not concluding, because endlessly generative of thanks and new improvisations of love) word on friendship:

> I love and am loved. All my tinyness rejoices
> That I'll have been a voice among your voices.[9]

## Sex—Hot and Cool

The most common association of love in much Western culture is with sex. To be lovers and to make love is to have sexual intercourse together. One's love life is centered on who one is having sex with, and similar associations go with "love affair," "love story," "love interest," "falling in love," "free love", and so on. Our commercial and social media, advertising, songs, literature, and theater are soaked in sex-related ideas, images, stories, and allusions. Beyond communications and entertainment, there are many other sex-related industries, businesses, and services concerned with health, sexual function, conceiving babies, contraception, abortion, therapies, beauty and personal appearance, dating, weddings and civil partnerships, clothing, clubs, and much else. Research and other sorts of thinking about sex occupy many chemists, biologists, medical scientists, social scientists, lawyers, doctors, teachers, economists, politicians, film and theater and literary critics, cultural commentators, and gossips. There is also the seamier, often illegal, side in pornography, drugs, prostitution, and a wide range of other sexual "services" and practices, and crimes of rape, sexual violence, sexual abuse, sexual oppression and manipulation, sexual discrimination, sexual harassment, stalking, or sex trafficking. Further dimensions are added to all this according to whether it is heterosexual, homosexual, bisexual, or transsexual. And it is easily forgotten that without sex none of us would be alive.

### Celebrating Sex

A "hot" take on sex must first of all celebrate it. Sex can be utterly ecstatic, sheer joy, amazing, satisfying in ways we may not have dreamed of, liberating, inspiring, energizing, the climax of a relationship and also its repeated physical and passionate renewal. The bliss of good sex can give a fundamental sense of fulfillment and well-being. To be in love and to make love with someone you adore and delight in, and who adores and delights in you, makes sense of the hype about sex. It resonates with all those love songs, love poems, love stories, dramas, and films that evoke the joys of lovemaking. O'Siadhail's "Matins for You" gives a taste of it, with the sex only hinted at. In *Love Life*, written out of nearly three decades of marriage, the lovemaking is more explicit, beginning in the opening poem, "Homing":

111

O Eros ravish and enlarge us.
Just to gaze, to listen, to mingle.
Sweet fusion. Carnal relish.
Break me again with outlandish
Desire my prowling Mademoiselle.
The arrow of our time discharges.[10]

"The Crimson Thread," the first section of *Love Life*, evokes lovemaking through all the senses, through moods and intertexts (Petrarch, Dante, Herrick, Abelard and Heloise, Shakespeare, and above all the Song of Songs), through subtle and daring description, and through classic and innovative forms of rhyme, meter, and assonance (in my rereading just now I have found yet more of these, including several with a pattern like "Globe," in which the first line rhymes with the eighteenth, the second with the seventeenth, and so on, and the sense chimes with the form). "Long Song" harks back to the Garden of Eden and interweaves lines from the Song of Songs with the intimate drama of lovemaking:

Fragrance of your oils.
*L'amour fou.* Such sweet folly.
Your haunting presence
Distilled traces of perfume.
Resonances of voice
Dwell in my nervous body.
My skin wants to glow,
All of my being glistens.
Divine shining through.
*Your lips like a crimson thread,*
*Your mouth is lovely. . . .*
*You're all beautiful, my love.*
Honeyed obsession
Of unreasonable love.
Pleased, being pleased,

I caress this amplitude,
Eternal roundness.
Voluptuous golden ring.
Sap and juices sing
Eden's long song in the veins.
Spirit into flesh.
The flesh into the spirit.
*A garden fountain,*
*A well of living water,*
*Flowing streams from Lebanon.*[11]

"For Real" voices amazed, attentive delight in the body, laughter, and very being of the beloved, the fresh intensity that being in love gives to tastes, colors, and the whole of reality, and the sense that there could never be enough of this:

A first gazing at you unawares.
Wonder by wonder my body savours

The conch-like detail of an ear,
An amethyst ring on your finger.

Could I ever have enough of you?
Juiced cantaloupe, ripe honeydew,

Slack desire so I desire you more.
Laugh as no one laughed before.

Vivid more vivid, real more real.
I stare towards heavens you reveal.

Yellower yellow. Bluer blue.
Can you see me as I see you?

Sweeter than being loved to love.
Sweetest our beings' hand in glove.

Milk and honey, spice and wine.
I'm your lover. You are mine.[12]

Other poems, such as "Exposé," revel further in the sensuous detail:

> O mind and king of thinking
> Unbend limbs come out to play.
> Abdicate a little while, uncrown
>
> A head with pleasures sinking
> In, our dénouement and disarray.
> A mellowing out, a meltdown
>
> As mute beguilements of attire,
> Soft options of yes's and no's,
> Incentives of an inner trousseau,
>
> Lingerie of gathering desire
> Scatter every slither of clothes.
> Fetish trail. Pell-mell libido.
>
> Throats murmur expectancy,
> Endearments gone beyond word,
> Sweet nothings, double Dutch.
>
> Babble and purr of fancy
> Uncage a reason's humming-bird.
> Pamper my Geist's temple, touch
>
> Sacral nooks and alleys
> Of lovemaking's stop-go calculus.
> Nerve-blitz and spirit-bond.
>
> An unzip of passion dallies
> In misty chaos glazing over us.
> Glisten. Doze in the dew-pond.[13]

The *jag of bliss* ("Sun")[14] is not a constant state so much as part of an ongoing drama of intimacy. This includes hesitations, anxieties, hurts, rows, misunderstandings, making up, the anguish of absence, and *green moments* ("Wobble")[15] of jealousy. And each lover acts many parts, as in "Play":

You, my all in one, my one in all
It's still summer, will you come out to play?
Let's make love inside the orchard wall.

Coy, bold, knowing, insolent, outré
Madam, goddess, nymph, vamp, flirt;
Play each woman you know how to play.

Strip me back to my core, tease, subvert,
Dig out, scour, clean, make me ready,
Flushing and purging any wound or hurt.

Unhead this wary head, unsentry me.
The ears of Cherubim begin to tingle
I come to my garden of myrrh and honey.

O vigilant gate-keeper wink one single
Moment, sheathe again your fiery sword.
Once angels we return. We fuse. We mingle.

Let's make love again before the Fall.[16]

Who could ever have enough of this? No wonder our culture is gripped by sex and its dramas, and that so many of us spend so much time, energy, and money on this fascinating obsession. But what about *the Fall*? What about the gone-wrongness of sex as well as much else? A "hot" take on it must also face its other side.

### The Other Side of Sex

The very elements in sex that can make it so gloriously good also have the capacity to go disastrously and miserably wrong. Sex can ruin lives. Wholehearted self-giving makes us terribly vulnerable. Just because it has such a grip on us, sex can be used to seduce, manipulate, oppress, abuse, dominate, and enslave. It can be used to serve money, image, or power. The longing for sex can fill our minds and imaginations and overwhelm our

115

sense of life. The obsessive, compulsive, addictive potential of sex can pervert relationships, families, and whole communities. And so on.

Need I dwell on this? We all know it well from so many sources. So I will not dwell on the multiple pathologies—personal, social, cultural, economic, moral, and religious—that sex is part of. Indeed, it says something about the prominence of this other side of sex that I do not know of another whole book of contemporary love poetry that celebrates a decades-long love life. In the midst of all the hype, we still desperately need encouragement that sex really can be as good as that, as exciting, liberating, and fulfilling as that. In a culture where so often sex is a subject of suspicion, cynicism, irony, embarrassment, scandal, knowingness, risqué jokes, "exposure," or political correctness, it takes considerable courage to witness to the fundamental goodness of sex. O'Siadhail tells me that his readings from *Love Life* can, understandably, be difficult for those in the audience whose love lives have been marked by disappointment, damage, or trauma, but the hope that such experience is not the last word about sex needs to be kept alive and nurtured.

How do we respond to so much sex gone wrong in so many lives and all across our culture? First, we acknowledge that there is a lot wrong and that we need to cry out for wisdom in this area. But where is wisdom to be found? I suggest a triple approach: a cooler take on sex; a take on life as a whole that deepens, lengthens, and broadens our life of love and tries to build a society to match; and, embracing all of that, a framework of meaning centered on love that can be trusted.

### A Cooler Take on Sex

Yes, sex can be as wonderful as O'Siadhail's love poetry shows, but let us try to stand back a little from that intensity.

I remember as a student the impression made on me when, with the college's archaeology and folk-life society, I visited the beehive huts on the Dingle Peninsula in Kerry on the Atlantic coast of southwest Ireland. They are small, round, dry-stone cells shaped like beehives where monks lived, probably from the twelfth century onward—an internet search for "beehive huts Ireland" gives a glorious set of photographs of them. In the midst of a sociable student outing, complete with céilidh dancing to virtuoso playing on a tin whistle, I tried to imagine the life of a monk in one of these huts. It was immersed in the rhythms of nature—day and night and the seasons. Fundamental for the monk was the rhythm of prayer through the day and the church year. We know the Psalms were central to that prayer, memorized and regularly repeated; how would he have experienced them in this setting? The Gospels, too, were central, as were forms of fasting, meditation, and other disciplines developed over centuries by Celtic Christianity. And, of course, there was celibacy: no sexual intercourse. By the time the beehive huts that I saw were built, the Christian tradition of celibate monasticism was nearly a millennium old.

Years later, at the site of the baptism of Jesus in the river Jordan, now sensitively restored by the Jordanian government, I climbed a ladder and went into a small cell carved out of a rock face that looks toward Jerusalem. This had been occupied by a Christian monk many centuries earlier than the beehive huts. Its setting was a reminder of two founding figures in Christianity, John the Baptist and Jesus, neither of whom (so far as we know) married. One of the other leading New Testament figures and authors, Paul of Tarsus, was also unmarried. The early church developed practices of virginity and celibacy even before the monastic movement began in the late third century. It is a strand of Christianity that has always been controversial, with the Protestant Reformation of the sixteenth century comprehensively rejecting it in its monastic and clerical forms, and it can, of course, go terribly wrong. But my concern now is with what it says about sex.

Clearly, sex is relativized by celibacy. The message of celibacy is that there are other things that can be more important for some people. You can devote your life to things that make it worthwhile giving up sexual intercourse and associated forms of physical intimacy, together with marriage, childbearing, and parenting. There are other desires and passions—for God, loving and serving other people, the pursuit of goodness, truth, beauty, and wisdom—that may lead into a life without sexual intercourse. There can still be intimacy in many forms (there are endless debates about where lines might be drawn); there can be close family-like community; there can be exhilarating collaboration in common ideals and tasks; there can be delights in creativity, beauty, and the stretching of hearts and minds in pursuit of a vision; there are many intellectual, emotional, and physical pleasures; above all, there is friendship. Love can enter into all of these.

The result is that appreciating celibacy is one way of getting sex in perspective. In its religious forms, it is a minority commitment, but extremes can illuminate the ordinary. It is important to remember how many millions of people do not have sex as part of their ordinary lives, for all sorts of reasons other than a religious vow. It may be chosen or unchosen, a permanent or temporary state; it may be due to age (children, the very old), illness or disability, lack of a suitable partner, the breakdown of a relationship, recovering from hurt or abuse, or dedication to a cause or work or sport or art or something else. Then there are those many millions who are in a marriage or other partnership in which the physical sexual element is either nonexistent or minimal (and they may find this quite acceptable if there are other satisfactions)—besides those in which sex is abusive,

118

coercive, manipulative, disappointing, or the topic of repeated argument, resentment, or pain.

Trying to imagine all the people (which may well include the reader) who fit into one or another of those categories helps get sex in proportion. But even those with what might be called a "normal" sex life (though studies and surveys regularly challenge our view of what this might be)—say, for example, marriage with two young children—will know how the role of physical sex in the relationship is easy to exaggerate. The total time it takes in an average week may be very little. Its quality may depend mainly on how things are going in other areas of life, how much trust there is, whether resentments have been healed, how much talking there has been about things that matter, how relations are with children or in-laws, and whether each has done a fair share of household chores.

A cooler take on sex leads, therefore, to agreeing on its importance for many people in some stages of their lives but also to noting its varied roles in the dramas of ordinary lives. It is possible to have a fulfilled life without sex being very significant. Yet in our culture, this is something of a well-kept secret. The pervasiveness of sex, as described above, puts pressure on everyone, especially on the life of the imagination with its traffic of desires, thoughts, feelings, fantasies, and expectations. One way of seeing this is that for many in our society sex is something like an obsession, compulsion, or addiction. It needs to be seen alongside other compulsions such as drugs, violence, shopping, surfing the internet, litigation, gambling, alcohol, or dieting. Most of those can be good, but their pathological side ruins millions of lives and sometimes whole families and communities.[17] The problem is that such a cool overview helps little in actually coping with compulsion. To find ways of doing that, we have to get "hot" again.

## The Larger Life of Love

The place of *Love Life* in Micheal O'Siadhail's collections of poetry is a good place to resume. It was immediately preceded by *The Gossamer Wall: Poems in Witness to the Holocaust.* That took nearly five years of immersion in the literature of the Holocaust, meeting survivors and wrestling with how to grasp the truth and make some sense of it. In daily conversations and as his first reader, I followed the writing of the poems as they moved through probing the historical roots of the Holocaust into the Nazi seizure of power and on through the work of death squads in Poland and the Soviet Union, the death camps, and resistance by Jews and others.

One of the most difficult sections to write was the last one, "Prisoners of Hope." How can life resume after such trauma so that evil is not handed a victory by the survivors giving up in despair? The key insights are that each one who died was *someone's fondled face*,[18] that evil thrives if love and trust do not, and that the best way of ensuring *never again* is to build face-to-face communities that can converse, say *over and over again our complex yes* to life and to each other, and celebrate together:

> A conversation so rich it knows it never arrives
> Or forecloses; in a buzz and cross-ruff of polity
> The restless subversive ragtime of what thrives.
>
> Endless dialogues. The criss-cross of flourishings.
> Again and over again our complex yes.
> A raucous glory and the whole jazz of things.
>
> The sudden riffs of surprise beyond our ken;
> Out of control, a music's brimming let-go.
> We feast to keep our promise of never again.[19]

That is a vision of flourishing that has room for many other intensities besides sex, and that breathes the air of freedom rather than compulsion—or, rather, that is a good compulsion, a liberating addiction, intoxication with *a raucous glory and the whole jazz of things.* This evil-resistant life is one with many loves. O'Siadhail's next two collections explore these from different angles.

In *Love Life*, it is as if the intensity of attention given to the Holocaust had to be answered by an even greater intensity of intimate loving. The need to have some all-absorbing recreation as a break from daily immersion in the Holocaust during those years of writing about it led O'Siadhail to learn sailing in the Irish Sea. The boating metaphors and imagery of sea, wind, weather, ropes, and knots fed into *Love Life.* They gave some of the language to articulate how sex can be taken up into marriage, so that it goes beyond a private intimacy. Two lives are joined, and a new family is created. The private act becomes part of a wider drama, a strand in the *criss-cross of flourishings* in interplay over time. *Love Life* traces the new couple's emergence into wider society in "Filling In":

> Early tentative encounters, our début,
> Friend by friend, coming out as a pair.
>
> The shock to find so many yous in you
> And still refind the you who chooses me.
>
> Slow transfer and knitting in of kismet.
> We move among others who move in us.[20]

At the heart of it is commitment for life. "Covenant" concludes:

> No barter. No pay-back. Gratis. For naught.
> I desire you. Just love me now and forever.[21]

This leads into a section called "Covenants," exploring the move into joint commitments, a house, meals, balancing two careers, hospitality, habits, routines. It opens with "Knot":

121

Right over left and left over right.
Or the other way around. Symmetrical plot
Of two mutual loops drawn tight,
The squared-off weftage of a reef-knot.

Double and single, a riddle of ligature.
Functional beauty sacred and profane;
A history of knots, a rope architecture,
Easy to loosen but tighter under strain.

Plied strength in our tying up of ends,
An emblem, one tiny glorious detail,
A sign becoming what a sign intends.
We tauten the love-knot, hoist the sail.[22]

Marriages and other long-term "love-knots" are, however, only part of the secret of flourishing and are not for everyone. There are other vital intensities, and these are also essential to the drama of living for those who are in marriages or other committed sexual relationships. The following collection, *Globe*, takes this broader canvas. Whereas *The Gossamer Wall* took a traumatic historical event and concluded with a vision of the face-to-face dynamics essential to flourishing life, *Globe* follows those dynamics in the world of the twenty-first century. Here love differentiates into a many-splendored diversity, embodied in friendships, teams, groups, movements, teacher-student relationships, and so on. "Clusters" takes the jazz combo as its leading instance while portraying a world in which these dynamics are formative:

Always our histories loop and so renew.
Schools, combos, zones of thought, a few
Tight clutches of friends, bands of dissidence,
Brainstorms, cross-breeding argument, dense
Huddles of players face to face that change
A rhythm's logic, curve our psychic range

To sift and fuse and rearrange progressions
That shape the mood of an age, jam sessions
Over time and the teacher-to-pupil baton:
Socrates, Plato, Aristotle on and on
Or chez Café Guernois Degas, Manet,
Cézanne and Pissarro busy arguing their way
Around their darker masters. Switched modes,
Nests and seedbeds, genealogies of nodes
As Satchmo Armstrong once played with King
Oliver and Jelly Roll. In musics of doing.
Yesterday's not today or now tomorrow's way
Which of course is never simply to say
That though there's no one way there's no
Yardstick and yesterday we sometimes know
Was better or not as good, just as tomorrow
May hoop either way to cobble joy or sorrow
In honky-tonks of being where rhythms swap,
cakewalk, ragtime, jazz, swing or bebop.
Dizzy's and Parker's chopped staccatos stunned
Munroe's Uptown House at 52nd
A variation become as weighty as a theme,
Fractured melody hovers above a seam
Of chord sequences in a six bar repeat
As accents land now on, now off the beat
In promises of process and substance blended.
Paradox of solo and ensemble in one splendid
Line that knows the moment of ordered freedom
When the brass blows down and yields to drum.
*What a man does with his life when it's finally his;*
Everywhere is local now exactly where it is.
Beyond a deadlock of perfection in notes that jar
We make each broken other whatever we are.
Polyphony of phrase, each open-hearted probe,
Clusters of goodwill in swap-shops of a globe;
Where music aims the music holds within.
The jazz is as the jazz has never been.[23]

The poem recognizes that improvement or progress is not inevitable but sees quality in every sphere of life being generated by collaborative clusters. This is where *histories loop and so renew*, and *the mood of an age* is shaped; these are the *nests and seedbeds* incubating our future, to which *clusters of goodwill* are vital. It is our world as an ecology within which love in this broader sense is intrinsic to every niche. Here are the intensities of good compulsions, which are the wisest way to avoid bad compulsions, obsessions, and addictions.

Other poems in *Globe* elaborate on this and meditate on the conditions for flourishing in our polyphonous, interconnected world. They raise basic questions to be faced if the primacy of the face-to-face and its possibilities of loving are to be sustained. What sort of politics can bring about *ordered freedom*? Amid the *swap-shops of a globe*, and given the *one-eyed market giant*,[24] what sort of economics can serve our flourishing, and how might it see with both eyes? How are we to clean up our *messed habitat, our greed-fouled nest*?[25] How do we deal with hunger, violence, war, abuses of power, and other evils? There is a prophetic power in O'Siadhail's poetic responses, sounding the depths of traditions that value love, compassion, and justice while fully engaging with the massive changes and complex dynamics of the contemporary world in order to improvise the next act of the drama.

I want to follow just two themes he raises: the issue of vocation, suggested by the quotation above about what you do with your life when it is finally yours, and the question of the basic meaning of life, raised by "Accelerando": *To move the earth, where's our somewhere to stand?*[26]

## "My Vocation Is Love": Thérèse and Arthur

Your "vocation" is your role in the drama of living. Vocation is usually associated with a career, often one with a strong element of service to others in it, such as priest, nun, teacher, nurse, or doctor. That is fine, but if vocation is limited like that, then the majority of people might seem not to have one. I think it is important to see vocation as embracing everyone. It is about each person's core purpose in life, to be carried out by him or her in their own unique way. That may or may not include a job or career that is traditionally labeled a vocation. In a Christian understanding, it is playing your part in the drama of living with Jesus. This may be full of surprises and not at all like what you think a vocation should look like.

In her autobiography, St. Thérèse of Lisieux tells of her discovery of her vocation. It is significant in itself that she was wrestling with it even when she was already a Carmelite nun, which most would have called her vocation. She wrote that "I feel within me other *vocations*. I feel the *vocation* of the WARRIOR, THE PRIEST, THE APOSTLE, THE DOCTOR, THE MARTYR. Finally, I feel the need and the desire of carrying out the most heroic deeds for *You, O Jesus*. I feel within my soul the courage of the *Crusader*, the *Papal Guard*, and I would want to die on the field of battle in defense of the Church."[27] As she meditated on these, she read Paul's first letter to the Corinthians, chapters 12–13, and the realization came:

I understood that LOVE COMPRISED ALL VOCATIONS, THAT LOVE WAS EVERYTHING, THAT IT EMBRACED ALL TIMES AND PLACES . . . IN A WORD, THAT IT WAS ETERNAL!

Then, in the excess of my delirious joy, I cried out: O Jesus, my Love . . . my *vocation*, at last I have found it . . . MY VOCATION IS LOVE![28]

As she continues to meditate this discovery is given a further dimension. All those high-profile roles she had envisaged before give way to a sense of her littleness, weakness, and childlikeness and to the conviction that "the smallest act of PURE LOVE" is worth more than all else.[29] This culminates in her praying for others who are little to realize their vocations in similar ways: "I beg You to cast Your divine glance upon a great number of *little* souls."[30]

The vocation of love is open to everyone and leads to an infinite variety of roles, scenes, acts, and story lines in the drama of living. It means that in God's eyes the most important things that are happening may seem very little to us. We need to try to see events in the light of a God of love. It is a matter of continual discernment to grasp just what this vocation might involve us in from day to day and year to year (which may, of course, include things that even the media would see as important). Thérèse's wisdom of littleness goes with that of Jean Vanier and the L'Arche communities described in chapter 3 above.

A while ago I was given a text that took this wisdom further still. It is called *Arthur's Vocation* and is written by Frances Young, a friend, scholar, and theologian whose son Arthur, now in his forties, has multiple severe disabilities, both physical and intellectual. She has written other things about him,[31] but this was the first mention of Arthur's vocation. She writes, "Basically, it's about appreciation, fascination, vaguely seeing yet not seeing, cheerfully being, just existing with a never-ending capacity for wonder at the simple things." This leads into a rich, multifaceted account of Arthur's vocation. Arthur reminds us of our vulnerability and dependence, relativizes the importance of language, witnesses to the broken body of Christ, and points to a wholeness that incorporates us with all our impairments.

But, of most importance here, Arthur also questions the individualism and activism in most conceptions of vocation. His dependence means that his vocation is utterly joined with those who care for him, and he is part of a body of love with many members. So his role cannot be separated out, but is intrinsic to

126

the shared experience of love, joy, peace, and other "fruits of the Spirit." This is even more radical than Thérèse's littleness and her "smallest act of pure love": it is a vocation to be loved in a community of love, loved simply for being who one is as God's child. If that is the basic vocation of each of us, then Arthur is our model. In the vocation of love, being loved comes first.

### Somewhere to Recline, Stand, and Act: A Universe Made by and for Love

Echoing Archimedes's statement, "Give me somewhere to stand and I will move the earth," O'Siadhail asks where this might be when the *leisure of change* is gone, there is a *new upping of pace*, and *so much of what we thought so certain slides* ("Accelerando"). John's Gospel suggests that what is needed first is somewhere to recline, to abide.

The climax of John's Prologue is a picture of Jesus **in the bosom of the Father** (1:18 NASB). The image is given various other translations: **close to the Father's heart** (NRSV), **[in the intimate presence] of the Father** (Amplified Bible), and **at the Father's side** (New American Bible). It conjures up reclining at a feast with family and friends. Elsewhere, John makes it clear that the "glory" of this relationship is, supremely, loving and being loved and that God wants others to share it: **"Father, I desire that those also, whom you have given me, may be with me where I am, to see my glory, which you have given me because you loved me before the foundation of the world"** (17:24).

What if the universe really is made by and for love? That is the daring thought at the heart of the Gospel of John. More than any of the other Gospels, John unites the intimacy and ultimacy of love. Within his Prologue's framework of God and the whole of reality, at the center is Jesus **close to the Father's heart,** a love open to all.

In John's world, there were many other frameworks and worldviews. When I spent four years studying classics, I was repeatedly struck not only by how sophisticated the Greek and Roman worldviews and philosophies could be but also by how contemporary they seemed. The basic options worked out by the pre-Socratics, Socrates, Plato, Aristotle, Epicurus, Stoics, Cynics, and skeptics were around in John's intellectual world and are still with us. Highly intelligent people still argue endlessly about the best way to conceive reality. After decades spent studying, teaching, and taking part in debates and conversations in universities in Europe, North America, and elsewhere, I have come to one obvious conclusion: people who are as intelligent as each other, as well educated as each other, and as historically, scientifically, and philosophically literate as each other can still come to fundamentally different convictions and worldviews. In other words, these ultimate questions are never likely to be decided to everyone's satisfaction by history, science, philosophy, or any other discipline or combination of disciplines. There are all sorts of ways of trying to win the arguments, new evidence is constantly being introduced, and intellectual fashions change (and are far more influential than intellectuals tend to think), but the idea that "all right-thinking people" are ever going to agree on such matters is unimaginable.

This does not mean that I think the exercise of critical and constructive intelligence on ultimate questions is at all inappropriate (I am, after all, a professor of theology!). On the contrary, it is vital that each worldview or faith, containing the basic convictions and visions of reality by which people live, be as intelligently and wisely thought through as possible. Our world is plagued by foolish, irrational, ignorant, and dangerous accounts of reality and conceptions of human life, and there is far too much foolish, irrational, ignorant, and dangerous faith. What is most needed is for each of us who has come to some conviction to hold and practice it as intelligently and wisely as possible and for communities and traditions likewise to seek wiser and more intelligent ways to be true to their convictions. "Seek more wisdom" could be everyone's slogan. This may, of course, result in some people changing their minds and their convictions, and communities and traditions, too, can go through major transformations. But the idea that there is some knockdown argument for or against a God of love, for example, is a fantasy. It is possible with intellectual integrity either to believe and trust in God as love in the sense testified to by John or not.

I suspect that in Western culture at present, apart from other religious traditions, for most ordinary people the main alternative to the Christian God of love, who creates the world as a theater for the drama of loving God and each other, is some form of atheist or agnostic humanism. This may in fact converge with a Christian humanism in many ways, allowing for all sorts of constructive alliances and collaborations for the common good. Many atheists and agnostics might also agree on the centrality of love and on much that has already been said about it in this chapter regarding friendship, sex, and the larger life of love embodied in groups, communities, movements, and the economics and politics that enable them to flourish. In other words, the "middle distance" of the drama of living, together with the intimacy of loving that helps shape it, may in many respects appear similar and certainly not contradictory. So what is the significance of the ultimate perspective within which **God is love** (1 John 4:8, 16)?

For John the significance is clear: it is about who Jesus is. He is not someone who fits within our prior framework, whatever that may be. John brings news, testimony to this person, an introduction to someone new he wants us to encounter. It is like the challenge of a new friend described above in "Widening":

Overwhelmed. Almost as if there's no choice,
A circle gapes and opens its embrace.
Hail and welcome! my new and prodigal voice.

John wants us to hear the voice of Jesus, and it is only in his Gospel that Jesus calls his disciples **"my friends"** (15:14). The voice of Jesus repeatedly says **"I am,"** identifying himself with the God he calls Father. Jesus is also the embodiment of God's wisdom; he is the Word made flesh. In John, there is no Sermon on the Mount, and much of the other teachings of Jesus in the Synoptic Gospels is also absent; the ethic and way of life are summed up succinctly: **"I give you a new commandment, that you love one another. Just as I have loved you, you also should love one another"** (13:34). Jesus himself incarnates this love by being the self-giving and self-expression of God.

So love is the wisdom of God and of creation. Love is not just an accident of evolution in an impersonal reality, though it is fascinating to question how to understand evolution and the God of love together—that is one of the many topics that comes under the heading of what was described above as matters on which the most highly intelligent and best educated differ. A key difference from the atheist or agnostic is that for the Christian the meaning of love goes all the way to the core of reality: there is no deeper or fuller sense to be made of reality and no broader framework than the God of love. To trust in Jesus is to live on this basis, to have confidence that love is eternal, love will never fail, love is ultimate. The trust is that whatever happens—suffering, misery, evil, death, disaster, trauma, loss of meaning—this love has the last word because love is the ultimate Word.

Within this framework, the most essential truth about each person is, *I am loved*. Jesus's archetypal disciple is identified not by name but simply as one who is loved by Jesus. He makes his first explicit appearance at the Last Supper: **One of his disciples—the one whom Jesus loved—was reclining next to him**

. . . (13:23—literally, **reclining on the bosom of Jesus**). The language makes a direct link to the love at the heart of the universe, pictured as Jesus on the bosom of his Father. The occasion leads directly to the death of Jesus for his friends, which is explained in this Gospel in terms of God's love for the world (3:16) and the drawing of all people into relationship with him (12:32). Then, in a passage about the beloved disciple at the very end of the Gospel (21:20–25—already discussed in chapter 1 above), after a reminder of that scene at the Last Supper, the mysterious openness of the future drama of love is suggested gently but firmly (by being repeated): **"If it is my will that he remain until I come, what is that to you? Follow me!"** (21:22; cf. v. 23).

This love—intimate, dramatic, and ultimate—has been thought about and discussed century after century, not least by St. Augustine in his exploration of God as a Trinity of Lover, Beloved, and Love. Here is the most obvious and encompassing difference from the atheist and agnostic: God as love, and the human love of God that participates in and responds to God. In John's Gospel, the climactic expression of this is in the final prayer of Jesus: **". . . I in them and you in me, that they may become completely one, so that the world may know that you have sent me and have loved them even as you have loved me"** (17:23). Jean Vanier describes this as "the summit of love." It is, he says,

> a unity that can in no way be achieved by human means.
> It is an openness and tenderness to each one,
> that flows from the deepening transformation in God.
> Friends of Jesus are no longer just walking towards
>    God,
> serving one another,
> they are *together, one in God,*
> *because God is in them . . .*
> each delights in the other,

each is a delight for the other
because in each one is seen the face of God.[32]

The vocation of love is to be loved by God, to love God, to be in a community of friends, and to be called to love each person created in the image of God.

## Conclusion: Befriending the Beloved Disciple

In case that sounds too idealistic, it is worth remembering the *slobber of dailyness* in the L'Arche communities inspired by Vanier (see chapter 3) and the lifetimes spent there in the drama of people with and without disabilities living together. Perhaps even more "earthing" are some aspects of the community behind the Gospel of John, as scholars try to reconstruct it. There is no unanimity, but it seems that it was more in need of the message of love than most. The first letter of John, probably addressed to this community some years after the Gospel was written, reveals deep problems, sharp antagonisms, and divisions, to which the author responds with an intensification of the message of love.

Yet this love itself seems to have had problematic limits in practice. In the Gospel, the most acute question is raised by John's account of "the Jews." Again, scholars differ greatly, but many agree that the frequently negative portrayal of the Jews in this Gospel reflects a history of bitter separation between John's community of Jewish believers in Jesus as Messiah and Son of God and the Jewish community where they had been nurtured and been at home. It is a family quarrel. The effects of that portrayal in the centuries following, after Christians had become largely non-Jewish, and more powerful than Jews, was to help generate and sustain Christian hostility and prejudice toward Jews, with often terrible results in contempt, discrimination, and persecution to the point of killing. This challenges any contemporary interpretation and application of the Gospel.

That was brought home powerfully to me by the Jewish New Testament scholar Adele Reinhartz in her book *Befriending the Beloved Disciple: A Jewish Reading of the Gospel of John*.[33] In four perceptive readings—"compliant," "resistant," "sympathetic," and "engaged"—she explores the possibility of making friends with this Gospel, represented by the beloved disciple. At the end she says, "I have not succeeded fully in befriending the Beloved Disciple."[34] She has gone a long way toward it, however, especially in her "engaged" reading, which has a good deal in common with what goes on in Scriptural Reasoning. There is much in her readings that I would argue with, but one of her main points is that such argument, together with "reciprocity and acceptance of one another's otherness," can be part of true friendship.

The acute challenge to someone like myself, who is a Christian friend of the beloved disciple, is whether I can learn from his testimony, face up to its limitations, and yet find the resources, within it and outside it, to inspire improvisation beyond it. John encourages this. The chapters of this book are an attempt to do it, helped over the years by Christian, Jewish, Muslim, secular, and many other friends.

Micheal O'Siadhail, one of those friends, has evoked in his poem "Session," through the image of jazz, the dynamics of daring improvisation. It faces the realities of deep difference, the wounds of history, and the radical suspicion that the fundamental meaning of history lies in power rather than love; it recognizes the primacy of the *face-to-face* and the call for *listening as never before*, and it is involved without overview in the drama of living—*without a theory or a base* and with *no map / Of any middle ground or overlap.*

Deep, deep
The legends and contours of every line,
Tune womb
Of our stories of who begat whom,
And as phrases part or combine.

So fine
A line between what's open and shut.
Proud horns
Above a shivering reed that mourns
What never made the cut.

Power's glut
Of power knows always what's true.
Somewhere
Against the grain, again the flair
Among a jazz's daring few

Some new
Delight in playing face to face
Grace notes
For a line that steadies as it floats,
Without a theory or a base,

Shared space
Holding what we hold and not to fear
Those bars
Where our history clashes or jars
And in lines unsymmetrical to the ear

Still hear
Deep reasonings of a different lore.
No map
Of any middle ground or overlap
Yet listening as never before—

No more—
Just hunched jazzmen so engrossed
In each

Other's chance outleap and reach
Of friendship at its utmost.

No host
And no one owns the chorus or break.
Guests all
At Madam Jazz's beck and call.
For nothing but the music's sake.[35]

Perhaps the main question for each day is how to improvise new love in pursuit of *friendship at its utmost.*

6

# Improvised Lives

*Timing, Aging, Dying*

Every day we make dozens of decisions about time and timing as we improvise in life's drama. It matters greatly how we think, imagine, and feel about time and how our culture shapes perceptions and uses of time. Does history have any long-term meaning across generations? Do we have vocations that make sense over a lifetime? What about our daily performance? What about those who are ill, disabled, very elderly, or dying? These are some of the issues pursued in this chapter, which, in line with its topic, requires a little more time than earlier ones.

## Timing

My mother got her first computer when she was in her early eighties, and some years later she copied me into a correspondence

she had with a friend, the American philosopher and theologian
Jim Fodor, to whom I had introduced her by email. He had been
doing research among old people and their nurses, doctors,
and caregivers and had found that practically all of them see
time as running out. Time for them is linear, quantitative, and
heading for death. But when he studied some previous periods
he was struck by different ways of experiencing time. There
was a recognition (often far more open) of approaching death,
but this did not mean that time had to be a fixed quantity, running down. Rather, facing death could intensify other modes
of time. He named three of these: cyclical, pendular, static. In
the course of the correspondence, my mother discovered that
many of the things that meant most to her came under those
three headings.

Her beloved garden was cyclical, as were the festivals and
seasons of the church year, and (with somewhat less reliabil-
ity) the recurrent daily and weekly visits, and phone or Skype
calls with family, friends, and caregivers. She had been a music
teacher and still occasionally played the piano, so pendular,
rhythmic time, the time of metronomes, was in her bones.
As what she called (in Teilhard de Chardin's felicitous term)
her "diminishments" increased, and her mobility decreased,
for much of the day all she could do was sit: static time. And
even her linear time hardly went in a straight line—mostly it
traveled slowly, and it could meander, take detours, change
pace, double back, or, with some short-term memory loss,
have gaps. The timing of such a life could not be done by clock
alone.

### The Many Modes and Moods of Time

It is worth attending to such ways of being in time, especially
in a culture that tends to make what is linear and measurable
the main criterion for "reality." It is not that the straight line

is unreal; rather, it is thin. It is impoverished as a way of doing justice to the many dimensions of time. As happens so often, the language we habitually use opens up a richer, wiser understanding. In it, time is active; as well as running out, it passes, moves, comes, stops, vanishes, stretches, elapses, slows down, speeds up, heals, brings to light, and does much else. Time is also passive; we take, make, pass, use, find, lose, share, give, spend, value, waste, kill, and do it. And those are only the verbs—there are huge numbers of other parts of speech to do with time, showing how pervasive it is in our experience and how nuanced our perception of it is.

Micheal O'Siadhail was for many years a professor of Celtic languages and linguistics before, at the age of forty in 1987, he risked giving up his post to work full time as a poet. After many collections that, on the surface at least, gave little sign of his academic discipline, in 2010 he published *Tongues*, an exploration and celebration of language and languages. It shows a fascination with the ways language pervades our world—all cultures, every sphere of life, each craft and discipline, the media, our relationships, minds, and hearts. Language speaks of time in so many ways. Many of our words are rooted in ancient families of languages—in "Mother" he traces that word back thousands of years and through many tongues to the hypothetical ancestor Indo-European. Then there are all the tenses and moods that form our ways of thinking about time. There are not just past (I loved you), present (I love you), and future (I will love you), but there are also commands—*No time for doubt . . . Kiss me!*[1] the recent perfect (I have just kissed you), the pluperfect (I had kissed you), and more, with various languages handling tense very differently. For us the future is ahead; for some it lies behind them, like all that is unseen.[2]

Terms that not everyone knows name ways of articulating time that all use. The optative mood expresses desire: "May I love you for ever!"—*how endlessly I yearn.*³ The subjunctive, the mood of "perhaps" and "maybe," explores the possibilities and risks of life and love. The conditional "if . . ." discovers

> A space between a future and our past. . . .
> If I hadn't loved you, God alone knows.

A sonnet discerns and enjoys the mysterious union of *movement and stillness* in *to love* and other infinitives that seem to transcend time:

> To wake, to love, to dance, to be, to do—
> Unmarked tense or person, unencumbered
> English underdetermined point of view,
> Non-committal dictionary headword.
> Both substantive and verb, a borderland,
> For Irish or Turkish only a noun,
> In Tokyo the subject hearers understand,
> While Portuguese lets pronouns tie it down.
> Undefined shifting in-betweenness,
> A spirit here and now that yet can soar,
> Verbal action and a noun's sereneness,
> Movement and stillness at the dance's core.
> Beside incarnate person, number, mood,
> A silence in the verb to be, infinitude.

Throughout the collection, and through all poetry, there is the shaping of time through form, as patterns, rhythms, and rhymes fill and form time in unprecedented ways. The form and content together may make us long to spend more time in the sort of reading that was explored in chapter 4, as words, lines, and whole poems are savored, lingered over, returned to again and again, and committed to memory; we are led to ruminate, to make new connections, and to allow our imaginations, minds, and lives to be reshaped slowly.

## Left and Right Brain Together

We live in many modes of time, and these are complexly connected with how nature, bodies, and minds work. Too much focus on linear, quantitative time is dangerously distorting our lives and societies. Iain McGilchrist, who has held distinguished academic research posts in both English literature and psychiatry, with a special interest in how the brain works, has reflected on how our sense of time is related to parts of our brain. The left hemisphere deals in clock time, dividing it into quantifiable units, homogeneous and abstracted from life, unfolding in sequence. The right hemisphere deals in lived time, narrative, music, depth, intensity, and imagining the past and future. Ideally, the two go together in a complex interplay, with the right in overall charge, but McGilchrist argues that in our civilization the left has become inappropriately dominant. The left emphasizes control, certainty, routine, calculation, detachment, practical usefulness, and technical manipulation. These are valuable, but are dangerous when they take over and downgrade the right brain's capacity for seeing the whole, engaging directly with the complexity of experience, feeling empathy, attending to the body and its senses, and appreciating metaphor, ambiguity, depth, creativity, nature, culture, and religion.[4] In these terms, Fodor's research has found that the sense of time in old people and their caregivers fits McGilchrist's diagnosis of being excessively left-brained.

How do we respond to this diagnosis? It requires both hemispheres together, led by the right's openness to depth, rich meaning, and imagination, but drawing on the left's ability to shape life through routines, habits, and practices. That sounds like a description of what religions offer at their best—but one also notices how much religion is gripped by what McGilchrist sees as the spirit of our age, seeking clear and literal certainty, following rigid rules, and competing for control over lives and societies. The interplay of left and right brain is, I think, best lived out

141

in a dramatic mode, where the "scripts"—whether Scriptures, poems, inherited ways of understanding and behaving, sets of beliefs and values, traditions, habitual practices, cultural classics, or people who are role models—are being constantly improvised on by us in the encounters and challenges of living now as wisely, lovingly, and imaginatively as possible.

Both the Gospel of John and the poems of O'Siadhail embody such "wisdom in the Spirit" in the drama of living. They also point to what is perhaps the most important aspect of time in any dramatic performance: the timing of speech and action. I see three main aspects of timing: having a sense of the larger drama, our own biographical or vocational drama, and the art of timing day by day.

### A Role in the Larger Drama

Timing is partly about having some sense of the larger drama in which we have a role. For John this is the drama of God in relation to the whole of creation, within which the particular focus is on the drama of Israel's history. Jesus is the fulfillment of the promise of that history; his time is fulfilled time, and John rereads his Scriptures (and, I think, the Synoptic Gospels and much else, including the Hellenistic culture and Roman Empire of which he is a part) seeking to understand more deeply both them and Jesus. The encompassing time is the time of God, which is called **eternal life** (for example, 3:15; 4:14; 6:40, 47, 54, 68; 10:28). This is not mainly about what we call "life after death." It includes that, because (as will be discussed further toward the end of this chapter) death is relativized by Jesus, who can say, **"I am the resurrection and the life. Those who believe in me, even though they die, will live"** (11:25). As Jesus says in the climactic prayer on the night before he died, eternal life is living in continual relationship with him and his Father, participating in their love (17:2–5, 20–26). This eternal love

142

life begins now and is inseparable from the ongoing drama of living with Jesus.

O'Siadhail evokes several larger dramas that have come together in shaping our twenty-first-century world. The Bible is a frequent source of imagery and reference. Not only the classical Western civilizations of Greece and Rome but also those of Sumeria, China, and Japan recur in his work. Within Western history, he has written of the Celtic tradition, the Middle Ages, the Renaissance, the Reformation, the Enlightenment, the rise of modern science, and late (or post-) modernity.

All of these come together in *The Gossamer Wall: Poems in Witness to the Holocaust*, as he searches out the origins of that historical trauma and its tragic timing and then traces its aftermath up to the present. The master image of this long view of history is that of geological cataclysm, earthquakes, or volcanoes and the shaping by them of the landscapes in which we live now—though always with an insistence on human responsibility for human catastrophes such as the Holocaust. In "Cataclysm," the signatory poem for the first, "deep historical" section of *The Gossamer Wall*, there is recognition of the trauma and of our complicity in it, yet also trust that there is still hope beyond trauma:

> In each human moment as in the time of stone
> Such build-up before a lava fumes in the cone.
>
> Cumulative time, a gradual hidden crescendo,
> Those lids of the earth's crust shifting below.
>
> Rifts in a magma chamber, a vicious blow-up;
> Bombs and cinders spewed from an angry cup.
>
> Sleep Vesuvius that once covered up Pompeii
> With pumice-stone and ash. Sleep and allay
>
> What fears we must both remember and forget.
> Sleep Vesuvius. Within us all your molten threat.

And yet. Another beginning. Another landscape.
Can the sun still sweeten even the sourest grape?

Shared scars of forgiveness, our fragile hopes;
The fruits and vines tended on your lower slopes.[5]

The imagery is taken up into the following poems in attempting to discern the roots of the Holocaust—in Christianity, the Thirty Years' War, the Enlightenment, the French Revolution, secular ideologies, the First World War, racism, fear of Communism, economics, culture, German nationalism, and more.

### Hitler, Jesus, and Our Vocational Drama

The *human moment* leads into the second key aspect of timing, what one might call the biographical or vocational drama, the roles played by particular people in shaping history. We need some sense of what our own role is, who and what we stand for and serve. We are shaped by the forces of history and by the hand we are dealt by what we are born into and brought up in—a family, a mother tongue, a neighborhood, a society, economic and social circumstances, an education system, a religion, traditional prejudices and enmities. Yet we are not just puppets of all that. We have some control over our core commitments and purposes, good and bad. We have responsibility. In relation to the Holocaust in a poem on Hitler, "Entrance," O'Siadhail ponders this interplay of what shapes us and what we shape, for better or for worse:

Convulsions in mother-earth, the trembling rock;
Blind forces, a chronology of fault segments.

Ground swell of history, compulsions of an epoch;
Part of, tied into, caught up in grand events.

Marionettes? And yet decisions made, the ties,
The hitches, the twists which ravel us into a plot

144

Too intricate to comprehend. The eye tries
To follow its loops but strays in baffles of a knot.

Implications of grand doings and small choices.
Both bound up and binding. A complex ligature

Shaping this history that's also shaping us.
Could there be a Desolation without Der Führer?

After two more sections on Hitler and his responsibility for the Holocaust (with several echoes of Shakespeare's exploration of a similar enigma in *Macbeth*), a fourth section begins:

A bottomless puzzle. No matter how we rummage
So much eludes us,
So much remains hidden
In shimmies and connivances, a stage-managed image . . .

A bestriding actor overcome by his own part . . .

It concludes:

Unwholesome radiance. A devious implacable will
Outpaces all explanation.
The black sun shines.
Quantum leap in some darker mystery of evil.[6]

John's vocational drama is a mystery of goodness and love, centered on Jesus and his awareness of being sent by God. Early on, Jesus tells his mother: **"My hour has not yet come"** (2:4). That **hour** is referred to at critical points in the drama. It is the fundamental orientation of his life. Eventually, just before his death, he speaks of it plainly and connects it to how his followers are to regard their own lives:

Jesus answered them, "The hour has come for the Son of Man to be glorified. Very truly, I tell you, unless a grain of wheat falls into the earth and dies, it remains just a single grain; but if it dies, it bears much fruit. Those who love their life lose it, and those who hate their life in this world will keep it for eternal life. Whoever serves me must follow me, and where I am, there will my servant be also." (12:23–26)

**The hour** is the death and resurrection of Jesus, and he agonizes over it:

"Now my soul is troubled. And what should I say—'Father, save me from this hour'? No, it is for this reason that I have come to this hour. Father, glorify your name." (12:27–28)

What do you live for? What would you die for? John's Gospel answers those questions not so much with a "what" as a "who." Will you take part in the drama of living with Jesus if it means giving up much or even dying? The radicality is underlined by the extreme language—**hate their life.** Jesus can also say, **"I came that they may have life, and have it abundantly"** (10:10). But there is an utter realism about death, evil, and everything else that threatens fullness of life and love.

This is the sort of truth that tens of millions of alcoholics who are part of Alcoholics Anonymous know in their personal lives: there has to be a death to alcohol and an affirmation of something or someone greater. The sequence of the Twelve Steps is uncompromising: "We admitted we were powerless over alcohol—that our lives had become unmanageable" (step 1); then "Came to believe that a Power greater than ourselves could restore us to sanity" (step 2); then "Made a decision to turn our will and our lives over to the care of God as we understood God" (step 3); then "Made a searching and fearless moral inventory of ourselves" (step 4); then "Admitted to God, to ourselves and to another human being the exact nature of our wrongs" (step 5); then "Were entirely ready to have God remove all of these defects of character" (step 6); then "Humbly asked Him to remove our shortcomings" (step 7); then "Made a list of all persons we had harmed, and became willing to make amends to them all" (step 8); then "Made direct amends to such people wherever possible, except when to do so would injure them or others" (step 9); then "Continued to take personal inventory and when we were wrong promptly admitted it" (step 10); then "Sought through prayer and meditation to improve our conscious contact with God, as we understood God, praying only for knowledge of God's will for us and the power to carry that out" (step 11); and finally "Having had a spiritual awakening as a result of these steps, we tried to carry this message to alcoholics, and to practice these principles in all our affairs" (step 12).[7]

Very different, yet comparable, radical challenges are faced by the tens of millions of people around the world who suffer persecution for their faith: is it worth sacrificing social acceptance, a job, my children's education, even my life?

In John's account, Jesus soon afterward compares his **hour** to a woman's **hour** of childbirth for the sake of a new life:

> "When a woman is in labor, she has pain, because her hour has come. But when her child is born, she no longer remembers the anguish because of the joy of having brought a human being into the world. So you have pain now; but I will see you again, and your hearts will rejoice, and no one will take your joy from you." (16:21–22)

What and who we give our lives to and for is our responsibility amid all the pressures, historical forces, and competing attractions.

### Daily Performance and the Art of Timing

There is the third and most obvious aspect of timing—in our day-to-day performance. There are new events, smaller and greater: how do we respond? There are tasks to be done, people to meet, judgments and decisions to be made, mistakes to be set right, awkward situations to be faced, a to-do list to be ticked off, and the more important items balanced with the more urgent. In all this, timing is vital. As any actor or actress knows, a good performance is not just about knowing your lines and rehearsing your movements, it is also about split-second timing during the performance.

In real life, the equivalent of the actor's script is our sense of the larger drama and of our own vocation and the plans we make in line with those. The equivalent of rehearsal takes place in education, training, and disciplines of exercise, study, or prayer; in the routines and habits that result from them; and in trying to match our schedules to our priorities. But then there is the one-off performance of each day's (and night's) living and loving. The script and the rehearsal are vitally important—without them we lack wisdom, depth, direction, and the formation that helps to shape our minds, hearts, bodies, and appropriate responses. But how do we draw on these in the moment, when we have to speak, act, or suffer? That is about the quality of our improvisation and being "wise in the Spirit."

John has more about Jesus and the Holy Spirit than any of the other Gospels. In the first chapter, the Spirit is seen to come and **"abide,"** or **"rest"** on Jesus (1:32, 33). Then in encounter after encounter we see what this means in practice: continual improvisation in speech and action, with close attention to times and timing. Even while dying on the cross, Jesus commits his mother and beloved disciple to each other in beginning a new family life—**and from that hour the disciple took her into his own home** (19:27). The final encounter is when some of the disciples after the death of Jesus have returned to their ordinary daily work of fishing, and Jesus appears to them and springs the surprise of a large catch of fish (21:1–23).

That incident moves into the exchange between Jesus and Peter that was discussed in chapter 1 of this book. Under pressure, Peter had improvised badly during the arrest and trial of Jesus when he denied knowing Jesus. Now, it is clear that this is not the last word, that Peter is loved and loves, that his vocation can be renewed—and that it will lead to his death. For the beloved disciple, there seems to be ordinary life with the mother of Jesus and the task of remembering, reflecting, and writing.

O'Siadhail is fascinated throughout his work by the fateful words and actions that shape the lives of people, communities, and epochs and by the role of individual responsibility in these. Woven into the large-scale historical drama of *The Gossamer Wall* are the stories of individuals. Hitler spends an evening with Heydrich and Himmler.[8] Hindenburg does a deal with Hitler, allowing him to become chancellor, and O'Siadhail reflects:

> How nearly it didn't happen. Fortune's somersault,
> Blind worm of disaster,
> A blundering drama,
> Tragedy of this black knot somehow tied by default.
> Sophocles watches.
> The flaw. The downfall.
> So little might have brought a juggernaut to a halt.[9]

In Northeim, Wilhelm Spannaus and Ernst Girmann play their parts in the Nazi takeover of the town. The *everyday men* of Battalion 101—Wohlauf, Hoffmann, Trapp, Gnade—become hardened to their task of killing tens of thousands of Jews in Poland. There are acts of generosity (*Lulu offers a tea ration to a parched comrade*)[10] and courage (Blumenfrucht refuses to betray comrades through days of torture—*and when he screamed he said: / I will not speak, I am dead no matter what*).[11] Lewental risks writing down what happened in the Birkenau concentration camp and buries it in a thermos in the ash of Crematorium III—*a cache / Of testimony, resistance of a word.*[12] There are the tragic compromises people make to survive but also whole families killed for daring to hide Jews. There is a section on Le Chambon, the Huguenot village led by Pastor Trocmé that saved hundreds of Jews:

> Here the hungry depths of Huguenot memory.
> Jews? But we only know one human kind. . . .
>
> No time for idle compassion. A violent man
> bridled by love, Trocmé has begun to sow
> in the long readied soil of grey Le Chambon
> his stubborn mustard seed of quiet resistance.
> A stranger's face caressed. A door ajar.
> *City of refuge, lest innocent blood be shed.* [13]

Whether in the historic or in the ordinary dramas of living, we do have an irreducible responsibility for how we speak, act, and suffer. This responsibility may be very different from what those around us think it is (perhaps greater, perhaps less), but it is a fundamental reality before God and our conscience. Our irresponsibility, our failures, our wrong acts of commission or omission, our addictions and obsessions, our sin: these need never be the last word about us, but at some point we need to repent of them.

The timing of repentance is easy: it is always now. The timing and substance of the renewal, reparation, and reconciliation that usually need to follow repentance are more difficult and usually require wise counsel and encouragement from others. When these and other good things happen, it is time for the other act whose timing is always now: thanks.

### Shakespeare and Psychotherapy in Broadmoor

It was a little decision with long-term consequences. I had received a short letter out of the blue from someone I did not know, asking whether he might come and have a conversation the following Saturday about theology in relation to his own interests, which he did not specify. My wife, Deborah, and I agreed to suggest he come an hour before supper and to invite him to stay for a meal if it was going well. It was the beginning of a friendship that was important for both Deborah and myself. He was Murray Cox, a psychiatrist who worked first in Pentonville Prison and then for more than twenty years as chief psychotherapist in Broadmoor, a high-security psychiatric hospital to which many of the patients are committed because they have been convicted of serious crimes and are suffering from mental illness.

Some years before McGilchrist wrote, Cox had a long-term collaboration with Alice Theilgaard, a Danish neurologist and professor of medical psychology. They drew both on knowledge of how the brain works and on literature and how language works in order to inform the practice of psychotherapy and, in particular, the then-young subdiscipline of forensic psychotherapy. Their major work together is called *Shakespeare as Prompter: The Amending Imagination and the Therapeutic Process.*[14] In my terms, it brings together the three dimensions of good timing: the larger dramatic world of Shakespeare's plays and poetry; the biographical, vocational dramas not only of Cox and Theilgaard but also of Cox's patients in Broadmoor; and the day-to-day performance of psychotherapy in Broadmoor. Cox knew much of Shakespeare (and of the Bible) by heart and was also alert both to Shakespeare studies and to the dynamics of actual performance—he was an honorary research fellow of the Shakespeare Institute at Birmingham University and an adviser to the Royal Shakespeare Company.

"Prompting" is a key concept for Cox and Theilgaard. In the theater, the prompter helps the actor when there is a blockage, a failure of memory, an inability to take the drama forward, and the prompter has the script of the play to refer to. The therapist who can draw on the scripts of Shakespeare has immense resources for "prompting" a patient or client who might be trapped by their past; have paralyzing anxiety, guilt, resentment, self-hatred, or indecision; and not know how to go on with life. The prompting inspired by something in Shakespeare's rich world of characters, plots, and language can help to free up the personality that is "stuck." It is by no means just about quotation. It is more usually the resonances of imagery, rhythm, cadence, or emphasis; the sense of how a plot or character might develop; and the sorts of association that are generated through immersion in Shakespeare's plays in performance. "It is as though a 'full-stop' is transformed into a 'comma,' so that a previously blocked end-point becomes a point of transition. This leads the recovery/discovery of buried emotion toward the next phase of integration."[15]

Out of hundreds of vivid examples from what Cox calls the "therapeutic space" of Broadmoor, I offer just one of special relevance to this chapter.

> Members were reflecting upon the fact that the time spent in therapy ran concurrently with the unknown duration of the sequential time of a hospital order [the court had not set any limit to their term in Broadmoor]:
> "We are doing time *and* psychotherapy."
> "In prisons they 'do time.'"
> "We do both at the same time."
> "Surely it *always* takes time to do psychotherapy."

[Cox and Theilgaard comment:] Here, with crystal clarity, is encapsulated much of the perennial debate about psychotherapy. Patients often want "quick" therapy, like hypnosis, because "it does not take time." *Catharsis* can be profound but brief, but its effects rarely endure, so that repetition is necessary. Deep interpretative psychotherapy takes time, because it depends on a psychological process known as "working through." And this can never be rushed.

With his many-faceted view of time, Shakespeare helps to free us from overwhelming dependence on digital clock-time, which now tyrannizes western culture. . . . Fortunately, there are those, Bachelard among them, who hold the view that "time should be round." Shakespeare is there too:

> Time is come round
> And where I did begin, there I shall end.
> My life is run his compass. (*Julius Caesar* V.3.23)

Hotspur seized the phenomenon of time in all its richness. For him time *takes survey of all the world* (*Henry IV* V.4.81), and time appears in many guises and disguises. Time is creator, destroyer, revealer, unfolder, ally, messenger, hero or villain.[16]

Sadly, Cox died suddenly at the age of sixty-six when a minor operation went wrong. His obituary in *The Independent* newspaper said:

Alice Theilgaard has used the Danish word "musisk" of him, meaning "a man of all the muses." It was this multifaceted, imaginative profundity, energised by huge enthusiasm, which let him constantly make new connections, cross boundaries, explore the many layers of a good metaphor, and improvise gloriously in conversation, lecturing or at the piano. The eyes twinkled, the humour danced and played with words, and the timing was always superb.[17]

That is the spirit of daily improvisation, as we pursue our vocations of love in the drama of living, drawing on the resources of the larger drama and of all that has played a part in our own formation.

## Aging

Aging is simply carrying on with the drama of living and loving. I asked a friend in her seventies, Margie Tolstoy, what her thoughts were on aging, and she said, "The secret is trying to grow wiser—otherwise it can be awful."[18] We see foolish and fearful attitudes to aging all around us; this chapter is my attempt to seek wisdom about it. Much of what has been said about the drama of living and becoming wise in the Spirit is relevant to any phase of life, to schoolchild, student, young adult, middle aged, or elderly and also, I hope, to those whose movement through those stages is affected by severe disability or other disadvantage.

### Middle Age and Beyond

Moving into and beyond middle age does, as Margie said, emphasize the need for wisdom and coming to terms with ourselves and what matters most to us. O'Siadhail at age fifty takes stock of his life in "Tapestry." He looks back at his *high and mighty youth* and its dismissal of the past, its meanings, and its people. Apparently of no significance in a cosmic perspective—*The time of quasars. . . . How we count in light-years for so little*—yet he takes the risk that there is something wiser and truer than the *black hole of despair. Meaningless whirlabout.*

So he relearns *the inching tempo of creation*, affirming *some steadier love*, and the *sweated delight of vocation*. Above all, there is the sense of community with the dead as well as the living, with *our ancients, saints, women loved, fathers sought,* and *friends who grew so slowly mine,* and alertness to the importance of each of those *tiny dovetailed threads in tapestries of being.*

That they should simply vanish. Could that be?
A great divide. Cessation. An absolute cut-off.
Somehow they still encompass and transfigure me.

And so to ponder again rituals of our ancients.
Skull in the rafters. Urned bones. Or nearer us,
Pilgrims travelling barefoot to graves of saints.

Our shapers always with us. Hovering. Hands-off.
Both here and hereafterwards. Shuttling spirits,
Invisible negotiations in hints and traces of love.

An embrace. A caress. Just the memory of a kiss.
Tiny dovetailed threads in tapestries of being.
An eternity or two to unravel an inch of this.

The moment of a single weft. The time of quasars.
Be with me now all beloved and bequeathed gone.
I must grow older among my saints and stars.

Glory to the fallen, all gone on
And what loves refuse oblivion,
So loomed and knotted in a history
Textures shuttled through in me.
My women loved, the fathers sought,
All movers, shakers of my thought.
A music heard, the good word said,
Wound in the tensions of a thread:
Complex now the pattern and design,
My friends who grew so slowly mine
And the more mine even though you
Looped around and out of view.
The pull and ease of every thread
Traffic between my living and my dead,
Behind in hidden warps of tapestry
The loved and gone are steadying me.
In all the daily weft and stain,
Ridge in my fabric, still the grain,
Though long woven over and undergone,
Glory to the fallen, all gone on.

So many lives gone on, woven into history.
Combed and subsumed. So many unnamed to whom
We owe the achieved or changed. Small refinements,
Picks of threads gathered into one tapestry
Of time. Minutiae. Infinite detail of obedience.
Painstaking millennia over a low-warp loom.

How we count in light-years for so little.
Of course, our high and mighty youth said no.
Black hole of despair. Meaningless whirlabout.
Let the gone be gone! Words too dry and brittle
Had begun to falter. Nib of ecstasy peter out.
A last breaking down. An emptying out of ego.

Only again to learn the inching tempo of creation.
No longer the darks or sudden hankered ecstasy,
Some steadier love makes all us weavers peers,
A surety in praise, sweated delight of vocation.
In just two hundred and twenty five million years
Our sun revolves once around the centre of a galaxy.

Nothing and everything. Blind journeys to perfection.
Those Beauvais tapestries, their grain close and fine
Up to forty threads an inch. Now humble and sharp,
This nib earns its slower ecstasies of reflection.
In mirrors lowered through a still unwoven warp,
The weaver's tilted glimpses of ripening design.[19]

That final picture is of the weavers working on a loom where
only the back of the tapestry can be seen but occasionally lowering a mirror to see from the front how the design is coming on.
The design of the poem has developed, too, from the three-line
stanzas of the first section, through the rhyming couplets of the
second, to the more complex six-line stanzas of the third, with
their *a b c a c b* rhyming and a good deal of internal assonance
and alliteration. The *ripening design* of a life likewise usually
complexifies with age.

156

## Ill-Health and the Community of the Weaker and Stronger

Increasing ill-health is for many people the main problem with growing older. Micheal O'Siadhail faced this when his wife, Bríd, was diagnosed with Parkinson's disease. Some years later he wrote "Parkinson's":

1

Stealthily. One day that quiver in your ring
Finger. Or my impatience at your squiggling

Such illegible notes. Just your astonishment
Noticing the absence of an old lineament.

Once speedy genes, high-geared and fleet;
At twelve the school's swiftest athlete.

The oils of movement slower to lubricate.
Stiffness, a tremor, that off-balance gait.

A specialist confirms Parkinson's disease.
Failing dopamine. The brain's vagaries.

Then moments of denial. Again so strong
And confident: Those doctors got it wrong.

Your fright is pleading with me to agree.
I bat for time: Maybe, we'll have to see.

What can I do? These arms enfold you.
No matter what, I have and hold you.

And so you must travel painful spendthrift
Windings of acceptance. Giving turns gift.

Together. But is there a closer closeness?
Yet another shift in love's long process.

2

Flustered now by stress,
A need for time,

Days planned, a gentler pace;
Any breeze shivers in your limbs,
My aspen mistress.

Hardy, deep-rooted, light-loving
You learn to endure.
Pioneer tree in fallow or clearing.
A random sigh flutters in your leaves:
*O God, I'm tired of shaking*

3

Often I wake early to taps on my pillow.
Last evening's tablet at the end of its tether
Your forefinger begins its morning tremolo
As if counting in sleep hours lain together.
I think at first you'd pitied an over eagerness,
My jittery hand that spilled half your coffee;
A headstrong giant-killer wobbly and nervous
That slowly over time you'd steadied in me.
Blurs and transfers between fellow travellers.
I couldn't but see your half flirtatious sidelong
Glance at me that both asks and reassures:
*Even if I shake I think my spirit is young?*

Our years side by side tongued and grooved.
A face is beautiful once a face is loved.[20]

The unsettling effect of the illness is mirrored in the form. It begins with regular rhyming couplets, but the middle section has lines of uneven length with some half-rhymes (*stress/pace* and *time/limbs*). The final sonnet begins with four lines of regular rhyming, but then *eagerness* does not quite rhyme with *nervous*, nor *sidelong* with *young*, nor *grooved* with *loved*. Like an aspen tree, Bríd is *hardy, deep-rooted, light-loving*; the sonnet form, too, shakes but endures.

But the marriage does not shake. This is not because the strong, healthy Micheal takes care of the weak, ill Bríd. There is not only a reaffirmation of marriage vows—*No matter what, I have and hold you*—and of the *years side by side tongued and grooved*. There is also a continuing mutuality in planning a life with *a gentler pace* and in the half flirtatious nonverbal asking and reassuring. Perhaps most striking is that—the marriage commitment being taken for granted—the fundamental question is, *But is there a closer closeness?* This new event in their marriage drama is *Yet another shift in love's long process*. For the poet the event is taken up into a love language resonant with Parkinson's—*My aspen mistress!* The Parkinson's shaking even inspires gratitude for the way Bríd has steadied him over the years in the areas where he has been *wobbly and nervous*.

This is no one-way caring of the strong for the weak. Bríd's illness evokes a compassionate love that is not at all condescending but deepens the two-way relationship while being realistic about the change that has happened. The realism that is needed to face illness as one ages has many dimensions, several of which are here. There is the sadness of remembering active, healthy years—*At twelve the school's swiftest athlete*. There is medical knowledge and help—*A specialist confirms Parkinson's disease / Failing dopamine*. There is psychological insight and sensitivity—*moments of denial. . . . I bat for time. . . . And so you must travel painful spendthrift / Windings of acceptance*. Daily life is reordered to take account of the illness. Marriage vows take on new content, and gratitude for the relationship wells up as *giving turns gift* and the early days are recalled—*I think at first. . . .* None of this can avoid the stark fact that there is pain and suffering—*You learn to endure*. Yet there is also the mystery of aging on which so many remark—*I think my spirit is young*. (I suspect that the age of that *young* is different for different people—I think I am around forty at heart.) In the last line comes the conclusive realism: the beauty of this loved face.

This marriage is a community of the weaker and stronger who are in a deeply mutual relationship. It is not weakness or strength, health or ill-health, that is the crucial factor; it is *love's long process.*[21]

If, as the previous chapter suggested, we are part of a universe made by and for love, then a radical working hypothesis makes sense: *some form of this community of weaker and stronger should be possible in every sphere of life.* The worldwide L'Arche federation of communities of those with and without learning disabilities have already been a vivid example of this in chapter 3 above. Jean Vanier, and many who have lived in those communities, have been celibate (some by choice, some not), and there are also married couples and families. The fundamental form of love there is friendship, above all the (to most people) surprising reality of deep friendships between those with and without disabilities. But what would improvisations on such community between weaker and stronger look like in other spheres? This is, I think, one of the main sets of challenges facing our world.

In politics and economics, how can the capitalist system and market economics be shaped so as to bring about compassionate societies in which the weak, disabled, marginal, vulnerable, ill, and aged are not only "cared for" (though that would be a considerable achievement) but are also genuinely valued, respected, and appreciated, and are seen as at the heart of any community in which face-to-face relations, celebration, gentleness, and wise loving flourish? Already capitalism and the market work very differently in different countries. It is shocking to see how low down the list some of the wealthiest countries come on league tables that measure child poverty, health care, housing, educational opportunity, social services, and quality of life of the elderly. This is not mainly about shortage of resources; it is often the wealthiest who are among the poor performers, despite there being a great deal of political and economic wisdom (the two need to go together) about how to move up the league tables. It is far more about a culture of justice, generosity, and compassion, which together might be seen as the form love takes in the public sphere. There is, sadly, no shortage of sophisticated theory, ideology, and policy justifying injustice, lack of generosity, and hard-heartedness.

In each sphere, similar possibilities open up since the stronger and weaker are present in all. Can education stop making most people feel like failures or at least inferior? Can the media (often owned by the very wealthy and staffed by the well paid) genuinely give a voice and a face to the weaker, poorer, and more marginal? Must we abort babies because of disabilities if in fact they may be one key to a compassionate society? (I recollect Vanier reflecting that many think that most people now in L'Arche communities should have been eliminated before birth.) Can peace and reconciliation happen in the world's conflicts, or must they continue till one side proves stronger—usually at terrible cost to both sides? Beyond the human sphere, can we even slow down the rate at which we drive one vulnerable species after another toward extinction?

I do not underestimate the difficulty in finding practical answers to those questions, but the main problem is usually not in the practicalities but in our blindness, hard-heartedness, self- and group-centeredness, and prioritizing the pursuit of money, power, prestige, success, pleasure, or other such devouring idols. There are, however, many signs of hope besides L'Arche, and most of us will have our own favorites. For such signs to happen, it is not necessary for all to agree that, for example, my Christian conviction that the world is created for love is true. There can be disagreement about that, together with collaboration in creating signs of love and hope. Alliances across deep divisions for the sake of the common good are probably the single most important element in enabling the realization of practical answers.

In the first half of the Gospel of John (chapters 2–12), Jesus creates one sign after another, from hundreds of gallons of wine for a wedding, through healings and a feeding, to raising Lazarus from the dead. But this leads to Jesus facing death and then dying. Each of us must do the same. Our life inevitably comes to an end, whether we have been one of the stronger or weaker. Jesus was both.

## Dying, Death, and the Last Six Months of Daniel Hardy

"We need to learn in advance of dying what death can teach us."[22] In the retreat with Vanier described in chapter 3, part of the second week was a series of sessions with Sue Morgan, who works in Toronto as a chaplain to those who are dying. Her themes were "Being with suffering," "Being with the dying," and "Signs of new life," into which she distilled many years of experience, thought, and prayer.

We explored with her the rampant fear and denial of death and dying, embarrassment and confusion by death, the neglect of so many nonmedical needs of the dying, the yearning to be remembered well, the desire to forgive and be forgiven, the misery and exhaustion of being in constant pain, the darker side of medical advances that may intervene aggressively to disrupt and complicate natural processes even when there is no prospect of keeping someone alive, and the light brought by Cicely Saunders and her hospice movement with its sensitive accompaniment of the dying and its palliative medicine. Sue found especially painful the "emotional wasteland" and "spiritual poverty" in which so many have to die.

Through it all, one simple, obvious need of the dying recurred again and again: to love and be loved. One man with terminal cancer had told her: "It's not cancer I will die of but loneliness." This was not so much about having people around as having people who could respect his dignity, listen, and speak heart to heart in the search for depth and meaning and literally touch him with gentleness. She had found that besides prolonging life, and even more important than that after a certain point, the chief concerns of the dying are for deep attentiveness, meaning, touch, and the presence of loved ones. Those certainly came together in the last six months of my father-in-law, Daniel Hardy.

*Wording a Radiance*

Daniel (usually known as Dan) Hardy was an American theologian and Anglican priest who taught in Birmingham and Durham Universities. For the last five years of his career he was director of the Princeton Center of Theological Inquiry, after which he and his wife retired to live next door to my wife and me in Cambridge.

I had met Dan when he interviewed me for my first post at Birmingham University. I then cotaught courses with him, and we began more than thirty years of conversations that continued till his death. Six years into our friendship, his daughter Deborah and I fell in love and married. After having four children, one of whom has died (Grace's death is written about in *The Shape of Living*), Deborah became both an Anglican priest (at present, chaplain in Addenbrooke's Hospital, Cambridge, and associate priest at St. James Church, Wulfstan Way) and a psychotherapist. My friend Micheal O'Siadhail was at our wedding and also became a friend of Dan Hardy. Some years later, on sabbatical leave in Princeton, Dan introduced me to his friend Peter Ochs, a Jewish professor of philosophy, now at the University of Virginia, and we too became friends. Later,

Micheal and Peter also became friends. Dan, Deborah, Peter, Micheal, and myself are the main *dramatis personae* in that part of his last six months, which is relevant here—though many others were part of those months too, above all his wife, Perrin.

In April 2007, Dan was diagnosed with terminal cancer and given six months to live if he underwent treatment, a prediction that proved accurate. He was determined to fight the cancer and had a major operation followed by chemotherapy, which was successful in giving reasonable quality of life till very near the end.

One of his sadnesses at the beginning was that a theological work, long planned and thought about, for which he had a contract with Cambridge University Press, would never be written. Peter Ochs's response to this was to telephone Dan from Virginia almost every day of the six months in order to elicit and write down his thoughts for the book. Several times a week, I would go next door to talk with Dan, and it was both moving and intellectually stretching to be involved with his thinking during this time. Dan, Peter, and I had collaborated in the genesis of Scriptural Reasoning (see chapter 2), but this was something new for all three of us. At the same time Deborah too was going next door regularly to talk with her father. What Dan dictated to Peter, together with two chapters by Deborah, one biographical and one about her final conversations with Dan, and a chapter by me on "Living Theology in the Face of Death," can be read in the book we later published, *Wording a Radiance: Parting Conversations on God and the Church*.[23] Here I want to take a fresh angle on those conversations in line with the engagement of this book with the poetry of O'Siadhail and the Gospel of John.

### Our Double Time *and Dying*

There was one book by Micheal O'Siadhail that Dan read and reread during these six months: *Our Double Time*. Several times we read aloud poems from it together and discussed them, and Deborah did the same. He also spoke by phone with Micheal from time to time. Again and again the poetry and Dan's dying illuminated each other.

For me it was especially poignant because *Our Double Time* contains a poem dedicated to my father, and one of the roles Dan had played in my life, besides friend, father-in-law, colleague, and coauthor, was second father. Micheal had never met my father but knew the effect his sudden death had had on me at the age of twelve. It had been my first encounter with death, it traumatized our family, and it led into years of questioning and searching to make some sense of it all—I suppose it is one of the main reasons I became a theologian, which in turn led to Dan, Deborah, and Peter: *Out of this loss all our lives will unfold.*[24]

But that had been a fatal heart attack, over in a single evening. Dan's six months made me realize the wisdom of traditional prayers asking not to die suddenly. This time of dying was precious, every hour together to be savored. It was, in Micheal's words, an experience of *double time.*

One condition for this time was, of course, knowing how near death was. "Whatever Else" is about the wisdom (though the poet speaks only for himself) of telling the truth about their condition to those who are dying:

How it is, how long they reckon it may be.
When my time comes, tell me straight.
Please no fudging or playing along with me.

Earthling that I am, forgive me if I shrink
In dread, rage, refuse or despair.
For all my talk, forgive my shying at the brink

Of this darkest leap of trust my life achieves.
To yield before the mind can know.
Imagine an apple-tree that fruits before its leaves. . . .

> Tell me while there's still the time to mend
> Breaches or even ask for pardon.
> Whatever else please for my sake don't pretend.
>
> Just tell me gently. Then, love me to the end.[25]

Dan's knowledge of his dying, and his *leap of trust*, enabled the mutual intensity of the final loving.

Dan was a multifaceted thinker, and there was plenty of complexity in those six months. But there was also a fresh simplicity, and "What If?" names it:

> Can it really be, I wonder, so simple any longer?
> I know the layers of things unconscious or hidden,
> How in our brokenness we travel from dust to dust.
> And still. And still. Those times push came to shove
> From nowhere that warm embrace, the hug of trust.
> There's some bigger engine unbiddable and unbidden.
> What if, I ask, what if the only rhyme is love?[26]

It was the simplicity of love, and a new directness in talking about it, affirming that *the only rhyme* in the universe is with *love*: that alone rings utterly and comprehensively true. Deborah's account of the last week of his life, given in "Farewell Discourses," the final chapter of *Wording a Radiance*, is studded with quotations from *Our Double Time*, from Etty Hillesum (about whom there is a long poem in *Our Double Time*) and also from Dan, with love as one of the main themes:

> It's all about love. I want to show people, more than tell them: to try to awaken it in other people—not from outside—but from deep within them. That's what "walking with Jesus" is: look at all those "love statements" opening out of his meetings with things and people.[27]

> I think I am probably dying. . . . So letting love grow between us between now and the end is what matters now: just as it is in

life as a preparation for death anyway. . . . It's all about passion, you know, that's what it's all about: love, passion, the ultimate simplicity and the ultimate complexity.[28]

It was in that final week that "Peter was able to say for the first time: 'I've got the book: Dan has finished it.'"[29] Each of the "Three Wishes" that Micheal expresses through three sonnets in the face of death were being fulfilled. The first is for *a good leaving*. The second is about *rites of farewell*, in line with

> The half dozen words of that Jewish prayer
> I love: May his memory be for a blessing. [30]

Peter later prayed at the vigil over Dan's body the night before his funeral, and he also gave the funeral sermon.

The third wish is for an *afterword*—about being remembered and wanting someone to tell the story of this life and find in it *some overarching design*:

> That some will depart early, others wait till late.
> One by one by one. That someone will be first
> Among contemporaries who wove each other's fate.
> And someone lone and last. Is that the worst?
> For all its doubling my time is still an arrow,
> Something I know yet can't quite comprehend;
> That my sacred friends too will leave and go,
> That even a plot's richest moments will end.
> Will there be those still able to tell the story,
> A few to recall how my chapters were numbered
> Or how in the light of an end to begin to frame
> Some overarching design, this life's trajectory,
> Someone to shape out of the silence an afterword,
> Or to say this was one narrative's perfected aim?

The book dictated to Peter later developed into something more biographical, culminating in Deborah's account of Dan's death.

Deborah describes her father's last hours:

"I wonder what [dying is] going to be like?" . . .

And he answered very calmly: "It's just going to happen, bit by bit: it's a matter of going with it." . . .

Later that evening, having already said goodnight to my father, I went back again: "Just in case anything happens tonight, Dad, you know how much I love you, don't you?"

He answered: "I love you too. Double. Complete." These were the last words he spoke to me: words of praise, just as he had hoped.

From that time on he was unable to speak, although we carried on our discourses nevertheless, pretty sure that he was still able to hear. From time to time he responded by moving his (very distinctive) eyebrows and, when it was something really important to him (such as hearing the news that my brothers were on their way), and by mustering every ounce of energy within him, with a beaming smile. Radiating that "bright mysterious core, broadening and deepening, on and on and on. . . ."[31] "the fullness of him who fills all in all." (Ephesians 1:23)

The whole family was gathered—surrounding him with the "ordinariness" of life and love that was also very special—and for the first time there was the sense that somehow, "all would be well." Alone with him later, I said, "It's OK, Dad; we're going to be all right. You can let go when you need to."

We read a favorite poem together:

### In Crosslight Now

In crosslight now all faces of my friends.
Every minute still so full, so precious
A furious intensity of knowing it ends.

That everything happened just as it has,
A variation expanding the glory of a theme;
That I bear the mystery of my mistress jazz.

To fill with gratitude, even to soar.
That one swallow that shall not fall.
A caring less which means my caring more.

Each small gesture, every utterance,
The glances I hoard. Some love is mine,
And always mine. A peace. A radiance

I've wanted to word but can't. My part
My own variation shaping this history
Of a theme as though one narrow heart

Contains the fractured voices of humanity.
Rhythms chosen, riffs of light and dark.
Autumn seems so steeped in her eternity.[32]

That night I dreamed: "I am with Dad in the Oncology clinic at Addenbrooke's. I am critically ill and am going to die and so is Dad. It's not dreadful; it's just going to happen."

I woke early the next morning and went in to relieve the nurse, who had been keeping watch with him. I looked at my dear father, as he lay "bubbling," working hard for each breath, amazed at how helpless and vulnerable he had become: like a child laboring to be born and having to make the transition out of his own body. It was too hard: "Babies die when labor goes on too long—this is longer than any labor!" I groaned. "It's too long: it's too hard for him, God, his dying will kill him! Help him!"

And his breathing suddenly changed and then stopped as he "gave up his spirit" as dawn broke and the sun began to rise, streaming in on him, as we said our goodbyes.[33]

### John and Coleridge

Alongside *Our Double Time*, another text that ran through Dan's last six months was the Bible and especially the Gospel of John. John dwells more on the night before Jesus's death than any of the other Gospels, and Jesus's Farewell Discourses (chapters 13–17) were always there in our awareness.

These conversations begin with love: **Now before the festival of the Passover, Jesus knew that his hour had come to depart from this world and go to the Father. Having loved his own who were in the world, he loved them to the end** (13:1). They end in love: **"I made your name known to them, and I will make it known, so that the love with which you have loved me may be in them, and I in them"** (17:26). There is also **"a new commandment, that you love one another. Just as I have loved you, you also should love one another. By this everyone will know that you are my disciples, if you have love for one another"** (13:34–35). There are many other references to love, central to which is Jesus's statement: **"As the Father has loved me, so I have loved you; abide in my love"**; this leads into Jesus calling them **"not . . . servants but . . . friends"** (15:9, 15).

I had just finished one ten-year project that had owed much to Dan[34] and was beginning another on the Gospel of John, so that was a natural topic of conversation with him. The prologue to John set the limitless horizon: God and all reality. There was the mind-stretching intoxication of exploring who God is, always Dan's favorite topic. The early years of our friendship had reveled in that, resulting in coauthoring the book *Living in Praise: Worshipping and Knowing God*.[35] As Deborah wrote,

> My father never liked to talk about himself for very long: he was much more interested in looking outwards and discerning and recognizing God in the people and world around him, in the particularities of the people and systems he was part of. Quite early on I discovered that the best way to spend time with him was to talk about God. He could never get enough of that. "Here's all this" (as he put it). "How is it of God?" Everything was related to God: whether it was the quantum measurement of subatomic particles or the details of Western intellectual thought

170

or a Bach fugue or the hinge on a kitchen cabinet. It was Aquinas' *sub ratione Dei*: understanding everything in relation to God:

I want to explore things in relation to one another: the intensity of the Lord and his presence and action in the world. Dedicated attention to the intensity of God: that's the source of theology; it's not about any academic contrivances. It has a doubling role: to explain but also to invite deeper into the mystery. It's a form of prayer done deeply within the Spirit and it requires sustained inquiry in many directions, by testing the major theologies, philosophies and sciences of modernity.[36]

During his last six months, he was particularly fascinated by Samuel Taylor Coleridge's thought, and several times in our conversations he reached up to a bookshelf to refer to a volume of Coleridge's collected works related to what he was dictating daily to Peter Ochs by phone. Coleridge had been planning a commentary on John's Gospel as part of his *Opus Maximum*, and that Gospel pervaded his thinking more and more. When Dan was given an honorary doctorate in divinity by General Theological Seminary in New York just before his death, Deborah traveled to receive it on his behalf and read out a remarkable autobiographical statement that included

a tribute to the thinker who has perhaps more than any other been my teacher and inspiration over many decades, Samuel Taylor Coleridge. He engaged deeply with God and most aspects of God's creation—intellectually, imaginatively, practically, spiritually, emotionally and through much personal suffering. Above all he responded in all those ways to the attraction of the divine. He discerned the Word and the Spirit endlessly present, active and innovative, lifting the world from within, raising it into its future—giving us a huge hope in God and God's future, and inviting us intensively and unremittingly to participate in that, as we are drawn through divine love into levels of existence of which we can hardly begin to imagine or dare to dream.[37]

*Divine Attraction, the Cross, and Joy*

In the words, "the attraction of the divine," lie, I think, the deepest and most original element in Dan's appreciation of both Coleridge and the Gospel of John during these months. One of John's distinctive features is the description of the crucifixion of Jesus in terms of attraction. **"I, when I am lifted up from the earth, will draw all people to myself." He said this to indicate the kind of death he was to die** (12:32–33). It is the gripping attractiveness of an act of love for others. *Wording a Radiance* shows Dan developing this idea of attraction by God's love in many directions, not least in a radical approach to interfaith relations that he and I discussed in relation to the work of the Cambridge Inter-faith Programme. It became for him a key not only to the Gospel of John but also to the Eucharist, to the vocation of the church in a multifaith and secular society, and to his own death in the light of the death of Jesus.

Attraction to God never ends. Eternal life is living gripped by the attractiveness of God's love. Christians are interested not so much in "life after death" as in "life after the death and resurrection of Jesus," which relativizes all deaths. So the love that is at the heart of eternal life can be our reality before and after our own deaths. It is a love that costs "not less than everything," but whose ultimate mark is joy: **"and your hearts will rejoice, and no one will take your joy from you"** (16:22).

That is the spirit of the series of poems inspired by jazz in the section of *Our Double Time* called "Variations." Jazz allows for the individual and the group, together with a people who have known slavery, to resonate together in an experience that knows suffering and death but whose embracing mood is, paradoxically, a joy springing from love. The rhymes, half-rhymes, alliterations, assonances, repetitions, metaphors, surprise stops and starts, improvisations, multiple times, tempos and moods, and the whole poetic art of "That in the End" seek to attract us too:

Here and now and maybe. To play is everything.
Interflow of mind and emotion caught in the doing.

Broken tempos of anguish seem to feed our joys;
Unexpected cadences, a tale of twelve bar blues.

Moody solos. Unique. The stamp of one voice;
Then pure concert as an ensemble improvises,

Hearing in each other harmonies of cross-purpose,
As though being ourselves we're more capacious.

Music of paradox. Music of now and metamorphosis.
Nothing unearned. A trust unconscious and precise

That in the end whatever I become or am or was,
I loved my friends, I praised my mistress jazz.[38]

# 7

# Playing without End

*Wise in the Spirit*

This is an open ending. It is as might be expected at the conclusion of a book that has been about continually improvising in the ongoing drama of living. "Only End" is the poem by Micheal O'Siadhail that will now be improvised on, and as the final poem of *Globe* it has a similar character. It both concludes the collection and is about *playing without end*. Both of the endings of the Gospel of John are comparably open. The first is about the purpose of the Gospel being to attract readers into trusting Jesus and taking part in the drama of living with him—having **life in his name** (20:31). The second testifies to the endlessness of what could be written about Jesus: **But there are also many other things that Jesus did; if every one of them were written down, I suppose that the world itself could not contain the books that would be written** (21:25).

One possible reader response to an open ending is to take it as a prompt to reread in the spirit of chapter 4. I do not presume that my readers will want to do that with this book, but I do hope that they will join me in becoming regular rereaders of the two texts that have been drawn on in each chapter, the Gospel of John and O'Siadhail's *Collected Poems*. The following comments on "Only End" are written with that in mind and also to try to take further some of the themes in earlier chapters and to inspire improvisations in the drama of living.

### Only End

1
Music of a given globe,
Off-chance jazz forever bringing
More being into being
Out of history's tangled knots and loops
Spirituals and flophouse bands
In hymns and charismatic whoops,
In night-clubs' vibe and strobe,
*Nothing buts* now *everything ands.*

2
Our heads are ancient Greeks
Who think just because they think
A body's out of sync
With thought but maybe we relearn the way
Our mind can pulse to intransigent
Musics of once broken to play
Beyond perfect techniques
The livelong midrash of a moment.

3
Given a globe of profusion,
We players are no legislators
More like mediators,

Who extemporising seem to up the ante
To find the nit and grit that has
A universal image for a Dante,
An aim without conclusion
To play mein host to Madam Jazz

4
Playing without end.
Growling, wailing, singing Madam
In anguish and joys we jam
As Davis's almost vibratoless horn
Wraps around Embraceable You
Somehow original and still reborn
Swooping back to mend,
Resolving just to clash anew.

5
All time to understand
Infinite blues of what ifs,
Breaks and tragic riffs
As traditions wander into other spaces
Zigzagging and boundary crossing
In clustered face-to-faces
Commonplace and grand,
Sweet nuisances of our being

6
On song and off-beam,
Hanging loose, hanging tough,
Offbeat, off the cuff,
Made, broken and remade in love,
Lived-in boneshaking pizzazz
Of interwoven polyphony above
An understated theme.
The only end of jazz is jazz.[1]

## Stanza 1: More Being, More Joy, More Meaning

The form of this and each of the other stanzas is a strict set of end rhymes—*a b b c d c a d*—with lines of varied length and rhythm. There is also a good deal of alliteration and assonance and many resonances with earlier poems in *Globe*. The effect is something like that of jazz's combination of discipline, freedom and repetition with variation.

Jazz is the surprise, *off-chance* outcome of some of the most tragic of *history's tangled knots and loops* in the slave trade and the complex interplay of African, North American, and Christian elements. Earlier in *Globe* other music of the oppressed— the Irish céilidh, Jewish *klezmer*, Ainu playing on *mukkuri* and *tonkori*—have also been marveled at for similarly *bringing / More being into being*. John says of the Word: **All things came into being through him** (1:3) with further abundant generativity happening through his Spirit—**for he gives the Spirit without measure** (3:34). Both are testimonies to the drama of living as tragic, yet not only tragic but also able to spring life-enhancing surprises. In jazz especially there is the joy and praise found in *Spirituals and flophouse bands / In hymns and charismatic whoops*. And these have overflowed to enliven the more secular settings of *night-clubs' vibe and strobe*.

Then comes the meaning: this is music that helps us think differently. We need no longer be stuck with *nothing buts*. I improvise: life is nothing but tragedy; God is nothing but a projection of our imaginations; the human being is nothing but matter; the cosmos is nothing but a blind chance event; Jesus's resurrection is nothing but his disciples' wish-fulfillment; music is nothing but sound waves. Instead, we can enjoy the rich, abundant reality of *everything ands*—yes, tragedy *and* joy too; yes, inventive imaginations *and* sometimes inspiration by the Spirit; yes, the glorious matter of human physicality *and*, inseparably, a sign of meaning, an irreducible dignity, an image of God; yes, chance and contingency *and* also novelty, improvisation, and good surprises; yes, fulfillment of the disciples' deepest desires *and*, at the same time, the creator God free to demonstrate that life, not death, has the last word; yes, sound waves *and*, in their creative shaping, also passion, bonding, and meaning through and beyond words.

### Stanza 2: Mind/Body, Music, and Midrash

This stanza has utter involvement in the drama of living. Jazz's sheer physicality—trumpet, saxophone, clarinet, and double bass; the body's skills, the voice, movement, sweat, flophouses, and nightclubs—together with its spirit-transforming power, mind-baffling complexity and intense mutuality: these make sure that there can be no false dualisms of mind and body, or individual and society. This rhythmic drama has both matter and meaning—another case of *everything and*. John confronts the dualist aspects of Greek thought with a radical challenge: **And the Word became flesh and lived among us** (1:14). The risen Jesus invites: **"Put your finger here and see my hands. Reach out your hand and put it in my side"** (20:27). He also says, **"Come and have breakfast"** (21:12). This is *a body* in *sync* with thought, other people, and the Spirit.

Besides jazz, *klezmer*, or céilidh, the *musics of once broken* people also remind me of evenings in L'Arche communities when people with severe learning disabilities play percussion instruments, sing, or just move to music. They have far from *perfect techniques*, but this is music for the drama of ordinary life, enabling communication, bonding, and worship.

*The livelong midrash of a moment* could be a summary of what this book has been about. Midrash is a Jewish rabbinic practice of interpretation that does not compete with the "plain sense" (*p'shat*) of a text but improvises on it in relation to some

179

new context, intertext, issue, or event. It is what happens in any good sermon or other application of a text—yes, there is a plain sense, which is the meaning in its original context, or in line with rules for "literal" understanding, but it is also possible to spark new meanings by thinking this text alongside others, by filling out gaps or speculating on alternative meanings, and by stretching it to apply to new circumstances and questions. The midrashic imagination is constantly improvising new meaning at the cutting edge of the drama. It is the jazz of text, being wise in the Spirit. The classic rabbinic pioneers were called the sages, the wise, and chapter 2 in particular has opened up a practice of wisdom-seeking that has learned from them and from those they learned from and taught.

In jazz, *the livelong midrash of a moment* is about alertness to the constant possibility of fresh riffs, variations, and *chance outleaps*. To follow a really good soloist improvising on a familiar melody is to be surprised, delighted, and amazed at what emerges. To follow an experienced jazz group as they improvise together can be even more amazing as others sense how to join in with what one begins and then add their own innovations too. O'Siadhail describes it in "Session" (the poem in *Globe* preceding "Only End" and well worth reading alongside it—it is quoted in full at the end of chapter 5):

> Yet listening as never before—
>
> No more—
> Just hunched jazzmen so engrossed
> In each
> Other's chance outleap and reach
> Of friendship at its utmost.

Transferred to texts, that especially emphasizes the potential of reading with others. Some of the best times of my life have been spent in conversation or meditation around texts—this book would be unthinkable without those pairs and groups. Whatever the preparation that is done, the conversation itself is unpredictable. In the *moment* of insight and exchange, a text can lead in many directions, and new interpretations open up. This midrashic drama brings together text, past authorities, present situations, and questions—all that has gone into forming the readers around the table—in an abundance of meaning that can be thought and argued about. The length and vitality of this tradition, as suggested by *livelong midrash*, is performed afresh in *a* unique, unrepeatable, and unscripted *moment*.

In earlier chapters I have read the Gospel of John both in its plain sense and midrashically and have learned that partly from John himself. His own reading of his sources (although the only one we can be sure of is his Jewish Scriptures, especially their Greek translation in the Septuagint, it seems clear to me that he also knew other Gospels) is full of daring improvisations on them, starting in his first verse with his "Christian midrash" on the first verse of Genesis. Becoming wise in the Spirit is modeled by John throughout his Gospel, but, if his readers too are to become wise in the Spirit, this cannot just be a matter of repeating what he says, any more than jazz players want those who learn from them to reproduce every note they make. Rather, as the jazz player is looking for gifted improvisation, John is wanting us to do what he does, and so we are invited to perform our own midrashic readings, not least on John's own text, as appropriate for our *moment* in the drama of living.

### Stanza 3: Risky Improvisation and Abundance without End

Madam Jazz personifies an abundance of life that goes on and on without losing its fascination and intensity. We *players* are not in control of this *globe of profusion*; we are *no legislators*

/ *More like mediators.* We are in the midst of the drama and need to negotiate our way, brokering relationships and roles. We cannot expect either an overview or a detailed script but must ad lib and improvise, *extemporizing* as we go. It is *we* who do this, not just autonomous individuals, and even collectively we are not autonomous; we have been *given* this world of abundance and have the responsibility of *mediators.* As jazz musicians find themselves in the midst of a *profusion* of melodies and musical possibilities—and mediating between them to come up with a performance that works—so we too seek to shape as wisely as possible our vocations, families, workplaces, communities, movements, and so on.

We are constantly mediating between people, resources, and possibilities that are in conflict or tension. This always carries risks. To *up the ante* is a gambling term from poker, meaning to increase the stake you are risking before the cards are dealt. Can we increase our stake and even wager our lives on something that both rings true with *the nit and grit* of ordinary life and its many negotiations and also has something of the deep, *universal* meaning of the *Divine Comedy* by Dante?

Dante's epic journey through hell, purgatory, and heaven is a story full of the dramas of those he accompanies and meets face to face. In terms of chapter 5, it has the intimate, the dramatic, and the ultimate all together, and love is at the heart of each. The radical challenge of Dante is to risk following a vocation of love for God and other people. That is, of course, a classic biblical imperative. But Dante's way of imagining this vocation is extraordinarily daring. Stanza 3 (together with the first line of stanza 4—the open end of stanza 3 suggests the meaning) evokes what I think is Dante's greatest achievement: imagining a life of love, joy, and peace in heaven without end and without it being boring. Part of his secret is connecting the *nit and grit* with the *universal* in a face-to-face drama filled with deep, intense communication. Jazz at its best is a musical version of this, and its capacity for infinitely creative improvisation on classic melodies lets it act as a *universal image* of heaven without losing touch with the *nit and grit* of its slave origins. Somehow, when O'Siadhail writes of jazz, dance, feasting, learning, conversation, friendship, and joy, it is hard to imagine being disappointed or bored if heaven were anything like this.[2]

John too is about *profusion . . . without conclusion*: "I came that they may have life, and have it abundantly" (10:10). He piles up images of abundance: huge quantities of excellent wine for a wedding (2:6–10); "a spring of water gushing up to eternal life" (4:14); food for five thousand with twelve baskets left over (6:13); "in my Father's house there are many dwelling places" (14:2); vine branches bearing much fruit (15:8); complete joy (15:11; 16:24); and love above all: "so that the love with which you have loved me may be in them, and I in them" (17:26). Abundant life, eternal life, God's house, and complete joy—these cry out to be given imaginative content. Dante and O'Siadhail are in a long tradition of trying to do so. What Dorothy L. Sayers said of Dante (whose *Divine Comedy* she translated) could also be said of O'Siadhail: "The possibility of enduring delight is grasped and presented in a way that the adult intellect can accept."[3]

## Stanza 4: Anguished, Joyful; Classic, New

*In anguish and joys we jam*—this combination in jazz recalls the crucifixion and resurrection in John, the dancing and weeping in the genocide survivor center in Kigali described in chapter 1 and much of chapter 6. The dark mystery of evil, suffering, and death has no solution, but we all wrestle with it and live out responses to it. Some of O'Siadhail's wrestling has been evident especially in chapters 1 and 6. John's culminating image for this is of the risen Jesus showing the wounds in his hands and side. Three times in seven verses (John 20:20–27) John mentions these wounds: they are inseparable from who the risen Jesus is. There is no forgetting the anguish, though there is also joy: **Then the disciples rejoiced when they saw the Lord** (20:20). Here is a double realism of anguish and joy. Of these, it seems to be more difficult to do justice to the joy, and to keep both together in a way that rings true is exceptional. Jazz does this, a key instance of stanza 1's *everything and.*

There are three "characters" in this stanza: Madam Jazz, Miles Davis, and *Embraceable You. Embraceable You* (ignoring the lyrics of the actual song!) might at a stretch translate *agapētos,* recalling the unnamed disciple who has been seen in John's Gospel as a placeholder for each of us and especially the ordinary "beloved" leading a mostly hidden life.

Madam Jazz occurs frequently in O'Siadhail's poetry over the years, and one of his collections was called *Hail! Madam Jazz.* Is she being invoked here too or only described? Her role seems beyond personification and resonates with that of Mary the mother of Jesus (especially in Dante's *Paradiso*) or even the Spirit of God—see further on stanza 6.

The only proper name among the three is Miles Davis, whose life and work played out both *anguish and joys.* He was not only a superb improviser as a player, both as a soloist and in combos, but he also, time and again, helped to develop new genres of jazz, including bebop, cool jazz, hard bop, modal jazz, and jazz fusion. Yet he had a classical music background too, studied for a period in the Juilliard School of Music, and apprenticed himself to some of the greats in early jazz, such as Charlie Parker. *Somehow original and still reborn* gets something of that return to origins and traditions in combination with adventurous innovation. He knew about what in chapter 4 I call "classic surprises."

The final lines of the stanza, *Swooping back to mend / Resolving just to clash anew*, raise again the questions of stanza 3 about the conceivability and attractiveness of abundant life, *playing without end*, and heaven. Without tensions, conflicts, and dissonances the dramatic interest of life seems to vanish, and there is boredom (think of what is conjured up by talk of heaven as "perfect rest"). But jazz points to a way through the problem. It is full of clashes and resolutions. The excitement lies in how one leads on to the other and then into still further clashes and resolutions at higher levels and in new ways. So the drama of creativity continues, and a life with joy is imaginable without any taint of evil or wrongness. Something really good is also fascinating and attractive.

It may be that each of the arts, and each genre within each art, has its own ways of representing abundant life while intensifying the drama of living and loving. They are all adventures in creativity that can go on and on and on—*playing without end*. The challenges of one of them can more than fill a lifetime. Together they offer an image of eternal life. The struggles of trying to complete satisfactorily a really good poem, novel, play, biography, sculpture, painting, film, building, or symphony are obvious—and are followed by the blank page awaiting the next poem, novel. Then there are the difficulties and delights of reading, understanding and interpreting, critiquing, discussing, viewing, staging, performing, and so on. But this only covers the usually recognized "arts," ignoring crafts, hobbies, pastimes—just think of carpentry, cooking, or gardening as realms of endless struggle, innovation, and joy. There are also sports and games—they too are played without end. Through and beyond all these are the dramas of human relationships and, above all, those of love. Here, too, in the deepest friendships—perhaps supremely here—there are differences, clashes, struggles, and resolutions *without end*.

## Stanza 5: Understanding, Face-to-Face, Sweet Nuisances

How can there be peace and reconciliation across deep divisions? This stanza rings true with three lessons I have learned from my limited experience. ·

First, there is the need for *time to understand*. I think of two decades of Scriptural Reasoning (see chapter 2). Hour after hour spent studying Jewish, Christian, and Muslim Scriptures together—along with the overflow in conversations, meals, projects, and friendships—have transformed not only my understanding of Judaism, Christianity, and Islam but also my sense of how best to reach such understanding. I have come to respect deeply those people on all sides of divisions who labor patiently to find insight and wisdom and are willing to improvise new ways of seeking it.

Such understanding should not be seen just as knowledge of what is the case (for example, knowing about each other's religion or history). In the right sort of patient, listening encounter, new understanding happens—both of one's own community, tradition, and history and of others. This fresh light both illuminates the past and present and also opens ways of imagining and acting differently in the future. Indeed, one of the most important things I have learned about understanding in general is that it is not only grasping what is but also sensing what follows from that. We recognize misunderstanding when someone does not know what to say next or responds inappropriately; our knowledge of a culture is revealed by knowing what to say or do next. In the drama of living, the deepest understanding is shown in the wisest improvisation.

When things have gone seriously wrong between individuals or groups, what might be said or done next that might mend the division or at least not reinforce or deepen it? Finding "next words and actions" often requires detours through the *Infinite blues of what ifs / Breaks and tragic riffs* of history, open to learning to understand it differently. Without new mutual under-standing, often gained slowly and painfully, I fear for any process of reconciliation. Improvisation in thought and imagination are essential to wise improvisation in the dramas of peacemaking and peacebuilding. We are invited to recognize that the full truth is ahead of us, not already possessed, and that the best way to enter into it is together, ready to be surprised. Perhaps most important of all is not to be exclusively focused on mending what has gone wrong but to trust that there is an abundance of good possibilities for the future that can attract us beyond our present understandings and difficulties.

Second, there are the *clustered face-to-faces*. In chapter 3 I made a case for the pivotal importance of the face-to-face, which includes chapter 2's account of how *traditions wander into other spaces / Zigzagging and boundary crossing*. Other levels of interaction and communication are significant, but, from cradle to deathbed, face-to-face is where love, trust, and the most formative and transformative communication tends to happen. These are essential for reconciliation across divisions to go deep and to last, and, in line with chapter 5, my experi-ence is that, whenever there has been substantial progress in peacebuilding between groups and traditions, there are to be found daring, dedicated, and innovative friendships and clusters.

Third, there are the *sweet nuisances*. This beautifully vague phrase is an invitation to midrashic license. It does not sit neatly in any framework of meaning, any more than it can be contained in stanza 5—it runs on wildly to a new rhythm into the final stanza. From experience between faiths, it conjures up the end-less hassle over appropriate food and drink, which yet somehow, mostly, leads to humor and relating better. Or an obsession with finding the meaning of one scriptural phrase—not even, apparently, particularly important to the passage—that takes more than an hour and ends with five possible senses. Or the passionate arguments I have witnessed between those of different faiths, wandering far from the original point into uncharted territory, both the passion and the freedom to go new places enabled by a trust they could not have imagined a few years ago. I think too of a Cambridge colleague who represents Scriptural Reasoning in a juggling act and of an academic Jewish group that broke into liturgical singing to illustrate a point.

### Stanza 6: Love and the Unspoken Name

This stanza begins in the overspill of the *sweet nuisances*, with the hectic intensity of jazz that is both

> On song . . .

performing what has been heard before; and also improvising in multiple ways—

> and off-beam,
> Hanging loose, hanging tough,
> Offbeat, off the cuff . . .

In John's terms, this is Word and Spirit together. They pour straight into what could be the motto for O'Siadhail's poetry and for the Gospel of John, as well as being the epigraph of this book:

> Made, broken and remade in love . . .

That could have been the perfect ending (like John 20:31), but there is more.

> Lived-in boneshaking pizzazz . . .

Besides being a delightful rhyme with "jazz," and a literal evocation of the music I once experienced squeezed into Preservation

Hall in New Orleans's French Quarter, this could also be a new definition of the incarnation—or a glimpse of heaven.

The *pizzazz* is

> Of interwoven polyphony . . .

*Polyphony* is a lovely symbol for a pluralistic world.[4] It is about several independent yet *interwoven* lines of melody in the same space, and the space itself is transformed by this profusion of simultaneous instruments and voices. It is a musical counterpart to the plural drama we are players in, with so many parts, interrelated plots, and theaters of action yet, somehow, still one world. O'Siadhail's *Globe* portrays such a world.

In this book, much of the interweaving has been done through scriptural and poetic texts that are themselves resonant with other texts, forming a polyphonic space for thought and discernment. *Only End* is a good example of rich intertextuality with the rest of *Globe*—the *knots* of history, stories of the *once broken* with their *breaks and tragic riffs*, the face-to-face, jazz, and *extemporizing*. Such intertextuality offers a repertoire to be drawn on in our own live performances and an invitation to bring our formative texts into fresh interplay with each other.

We reach the first full stop in these two energetic, loud stanzas, to end the sentence on a muted note:

> above
> An understated theme.

It is rather like John's low-key second ending of his Gospel. To the attentive, understatement can be more attractive than emphatic insistence. The refusal of hype and loudness can itself be a way of underlining what matters most—less can be more. That second ending is the only appearance of the first person I in the whole Gospel, and it comes in a modest speculation:

189

I suppose . . . (21:25). It mysteriously connects with the **beloved disciple**, whose underemphasized role in the Gospel is symbolized by being unnamed.

Similarly, John does not name the mother of Jesus. Yet, as discussed in chapter 3, she and the beloved disciple are brought together by Jesus at the cross into a household community that might be seen as carrying the DNA for the church as a family transcending family. This church of the unnamed reflects today the hundreds of millions of ordinary Christians and others who will never "make a name for themselves" so as to be written about. The essential is being loved and loving in a community of mutual service where both the big names and the little can wash each other's feet.

Even what is arguably the most amazing event in the Gospel of John is understated. I remember being especially struck by Jean Vanier remarking at the retreat described in chapter 3 that the resurrection of Jesus in John is told through a series of little events happening to obscure people—including, in a key role, a woman, whose evidence would not have been considered as reliable as a man's. These are not headline-grabbing happenings. The event of resurrection itself is not described at all, only implied. Mary Magdalene finds the stone removed from Jesus's tomb and calls Peter and the beloved disciple, who find it empty. Then Mary meets Jesus in the garden; some disciples, and later Thomas, meet Jesus in a locked house; and in the last chapter there is a final meeting of disciples with Jesus that does have a surprise (though catching 153 fish is not really big news) but is mainly conversation after a breakfast cooked by Jesus. This is a hidden drama in which the most important thing is clear: meeting, listening to, and following Jesus. Jesus gently shapes lives in ways that are appropriate to each—Mary's grief, Thomas's doubt, Peter's earlier denial.

The quietness of it all is symbolized by the giving of the Holy Spirit, not, as in the Acts of the Apostles, with **a sound like the**

**rush of a violent wind** accompanied by **tongues, as of fire** (Acts
2:2–3), but **he breathed on them** . . . (John 20:22). John can, of
course, be loud too—the cleansing of the temple (John 2) and
the raising of Lazarus (John 11) are the most dramatic examples.
But the very fact that his account is being written means that it
is in the quietness and slowness of reading, rereading, reciting,
memorizing, and reflecting that he expects the Spirit to lead
readers into faith and truth.

There is something even more significant in John that might
also be connected with understatement and certainly has to do
with naming. This is about the most important matter of all:
God. It is an insight that I have only recently had through reading a remarkable work by Kendall Soulen.[5] It has implications
for interpreting Madam Jazz.

The basic issue is, what is the proper name of God in John?
"God" (*theos*) is not a proper name; nor is "Father" (*patēr*),
John's favorite term (used 120 times). Jesus prays to his Father:
**"I made your name known to them, and I will make it known,
so that the love with which you have loved me may be in them,
and I in them"** (17:26). What name is that?

It is hardly "Jesus," which is the name of the Son, not the
Father who is being addressed. It is tempting to find it in the
**"I am"** sayings, echoing Exodus 3:14: **God said to Moses, "I
AM WHO I AM"** [or **"I WILL BE WHO I WILL BE"**]. **He said further,
"Thus you shall say to the Israelites, 'I AM has sent me to you.'"**
Yet that is not a proper name either. The only proper name
used in the Hebrew Bible is the four Hebrew letters YHWH
(called "tetragrammaton," "four letters"). This is sometimes
rendered "Yahweh" or "Jehovah," providing it with vowels that
are not in the Hebrew text. By the time of Jesus (and for a long
time before, though we do not know when it began), this was
not pronounced except by the high priest in the holy of holies
in the temple. On all other occasions another term, usually

*adonai* meaning "Lord," was pronounced, and when vowels were added to the tetragrammaton in Hebrew, they were the vowels of *adonai*. There are well over a thousand instances of the tetragrammaton in the Hebrew Bible, and it is the only serious candidate for being the proper name of the one God of Israel. (Many Jews today will not even use the word "God," or its equivalent in other languages, but substitute some other term, often *ha-shem*, "the Name.") *Adonai* came into the Greek of the Septuagint as *kurios*, "Lord," as in the definitive statement of the tetragrammaton's preeminence as God's one proper name in Exodus 3:15: **God also said to Moses, "Thus you shall say to the Israelites, 'The L**ORD** [YHWH], the God of your ancestors, the God of Abraham, the God of Isaac, and the God of Jacob, has sent me to you': This is my name forever, and this my title for all generations."**

From the Septuagint, *kurios* came into the New Testament. So the oblique, indirect naming of God as "Lord" or "Lord God" was carried over into Christian usage, avoiding the tetragrammaton, YHWH, God's proper name. In John there are only two passages in which Jesus is identified as God.

The first is in the prologue, which says both that **the Word was God** and that **the Word became flesh and lived among us, and we have seen his glory, the glory as of a father's only son, full of grace and truth** (1:1, 14). Any "seeing" of God is indirect, which is evident in the statement soon afterward: **No one has ever seen God . . .** (1:18). There is both an identification as God and a differentiation as Father and Son.

The second is when Thomas acknowledges the risen Jesus by crying out: **"My Lord and my God!"** (20:28). Again there is identification—indeed, the closest of all identifications, in the terminology by which the Septuagint indicates the tetragrammaton, but this follows soon after a differentiation when Jesus tells Mary, **"I am ascending to my Father and your Father, to** my God and your God" (20:17). Clearly, Jesus differentiates himself from his Father. In line with the prologue's **No one has ever seen God**, we are not to think that Thomas is directly seeing the One named by the tetragrammaton; however, this one God, the God of Abraham, Isaac, Jacob, and Moses, has revealed Godself in a new way, and Thomas is acknowledging this. The divine freedom of self-identification and self-expression, I WILL BE WHO I WILL BE, has freely given the divine self in this Word made flesh. John is saying that this is who God wills to be, the God of Jesus his Son. And it is accompanied by the divine freedom of self-sharing and self-giving—"**Receive the Holy Spirit**" (20:22).

What is happening? John, more than any other New Testament writer (though Paul comes near), is rethinking who God is in the light of Jesus and who Jesus is in the light of God. The conceptualization of it took centuries before it reached relative stability in the doctrine of God as the Trinity of Father, Son, and Holy Spirit.[6] John's own main concern is not with second-order concepts but with the first-order drama. That, from the first chapter, tells a polyphonic God-centered story in which Father, Son, and Holy Spirit are all inseparably united and differentiated—a relational God of love and mutual indwelling. Its climax is chapter 20 as just quoted, and its fundamental concept is the tetragrammaton. This is the oblique, unspoken name of God that pervades the Hebrew Scriptures, the Septuagint, the New Testament, and John's Gospel.

As Soulen argues at length and persuasively, not to recognize that this is the one proper name of God for Christians as for Jews is seriously to misunderstand the New Testament, which was mostly written by Jews who took it for granted. He follows the sad story of partial recognition, misinterpretation, and forgetfulness that has resulted since the early centuries. But to recognize it not only helps in addressing (as Soulen does well) one of the most shameful strands in Christian history, the Christian treatment of Jews; it can also inspire a midrashic interpretation of Madam Jazz.

I have suggested that Madam Jazz is more than a personification of jazz. She seems to be more, even, than a pointer to the jazz-like nature of ultimate reality. She is certainly invoked by the poet as his muse but in a way that resonates with Milton, whose opening invocation of *Paradise Lost* combines the form of that classical tradition with the Christian content of the Holy Spirit. It is easy to come to the conclusion (especially with John as an intertext) that Madam Jazz is a way of naming God—indirectly, metaphorically, personally, and of course open to countless other midrashes.

This God is as female as male. As Soulen argues, the tetragrammaton is not gendered—the God of whom this is the proper name is an ungendered first person: **I**. John's God-language of Father and Son is strongly male. If in fact his pervasive, oblique name for God, the name Jesus makes known, is the unspoken name of Exodus 3:15, then Jesus's **"I am"** sayings should, in line with Exodus 3:14, be heard as indicating that name. This relativizes the male language without at all displacing it. In her now classic essay, "Can a Feminist Call God Father?" Janet Martin Soskice answers her question with a resounding yes.[7] But doing so does not rule out calling God by feminine names too. Indeed, such a rich mystery as God deserves to be honored with many names, masculine, feminine, or neuter. John also complements his male terms with a diverse symbolic language from nature (light, wind, water, vine) and culture (bread, wine, king, shepherd), and women play a more prominent part in his Gospel than in any of the other New Testament writings. He does not call God mother (as Soskice is happy to) or Madam, but his freedom to develop, beyond any other New Testament writer, the Father-Son metaphor (that it is a metaphor for him is, I think, the implication of the **"as"** in 1:14 quoted above) is given partly by his definite but *understated theme* of the tetragrammaton and partly by his trust in the Spirit leading into all truth. John's God is free to become fully human, and become gendered, but the same God is free to breathe the Holy Spirit into people who can then improvise creatively, pointing toward the God beyond gender in language that is both gendered and not.

For Soulen, the three basic ways of naming God are "theological," by the tetragrammaton; "christological," by Father, Son, and Spirit; and "pneumatological," by an infinite abundance of Spirit-inspired names. He gives a selection of the latter that he finds most appropriate across the centuries and around the world today. Among my favorites are lover, beloved, love; lover, beloved, co-beloved; love, love born from love, sent love; unoriginate love, love from love, mutual love; rose tree, flower, fragrance; sun, ray, radiance; joy, bliss, delight; Fatherhood, Motherhood, Lordship; the One who draws, the One who sprinkles, the One who seals; Almighty, fountain of bliss, river of raptures; speaker, word, meaning; primordial being, expressive being, unitive being; *sat, chit, ananda*; transcendence, self-expression, breath of the future; *dao, de, qi*; our rainbow, our ark, our dove; planner, performer, enabler; sun, brilliance, warmth; perfume, sprinkling, aroma; mountain peak, cool air, freshness.[8]

The point here is simple, despite taking some time to reach: O'Siadhail's Madam Jazz deserves to be included in any list of inspired names for God.

But having reached this point I cannot resist asking the further question, might it in turn inspire some trinities in analogy with those on Soulen's list? Perhaps the following, drawing just on "Only End": profusion, lived-in boneshaking pizzazz, Madam Jazz; host, Madam Jazz, playing without end; Madam Jazz, spirituals and hymns, extemporizing; being, nit and grit, more being; mind, body, relearning; host, embraceable you, everything and; aim without conclusion, clustered face-to-faces, hanging loose and hanging tough; made in love, broken in love, remade in love.

The last line is an open ending:

> The only end of jazz is jazz.

Jazz does not end. In another meaning of "end," how is jazz the purpose or point of jazz? This line can be read alongside the last line of the previous poem, "Session":

> For nothing but the music's sake.

Jazz for jazz's sake, jazz as its own reward, jazz as an end in itself: jazz has intrinsic worth. Parallels abound, from art for art's sake, truth for truth's sake, and the rationale for almost any craft, hobby, game, amateur sport, or simple pleasure, to friendship for friendship's sake and human beings as ends in themselves. Partly, these are protests against subordinating such things, and especially people, to other ends. Each can be used instrumentally, and that is countered by such slogans. Each can be compromised or corrupted—the history of jazz itself is inextricable from slavery, American racism, and commercial exploitation. And jazz, like the other things, cannot be carried on without financial and other practical considerations. But there is also a precious purity of delight, a freedom of enjoyment and creativity, that affirms jazz as good in itself.

This is both true in itself and a sign of an even fuller truth, as suggested by my improvised theological meanings of jazz. If Madam Jazz is allowed to inspire this sort of thinking, then there is no avoiding the ultimate thought to which she leads: God for God's sake. *The only end of God is God. For nothing but God's sake.* If jazz, or truth, or human beings are to be valued as ends in themselves, how much more is God?

I have come to think that this is the most important of all theological thoughts. **God loves freely and is to be loved freely—which means, for God's own sake.** It is often expressed in terms of God's name—God's full personal being—being worshiped, hallowed, blessed, praised, honored, adored, rejoiced in, delighted in, and loved. To live like that with God, before God and dwelling in God, with constant, generous inspiration for *the livelong midrash of each moment* in public and personal life, is to be wise in the Spirit. God's name is the highest stake in this drama of living. God has upped the ante in vulnerable love and in Jesus bears the wounds of the nails and spear, the marks of being *made, broken and remade in love.*

As the final poem in *Tongues* (a haiku) might suggest, this *end* is not only to do with the generative and ultimate meaning of reality but also with the freedom of *birds of paradise,* in flight and in song:

> In the beginning
> The word. So too in the end.
> Birds of paradise.[9]

# Appendix

# A Vocation of Love

**Bríd O'Siadhail**
February 28, 1942–June 17, 2013
Funeral Address by Professor David Ford
Church of the Assumption, Booterstown, Co. Dublin
June 20, 2013

Micheal has asked me to express his thanks to the Alpha Quartet, who have played so magnificently. He also warmly welcomes President Higgins's aide-de-camp, Colonel Brendan McAndrew.

● ● ●

When I asked Barry Hickey, Micheal's niece Sinéad's husband, to whom we owe great gratitude for the organization of this funeral and everything connected with it, how on earth you could describe Bríd, he simply said, "Stand in front of the portrait." It's the one you have in front of you, the portrait painted by Mick O'Dea, and photographed this week by Gillian Buckley. As soon as it was finished in 2009, Micheal sent me photographs of it by email, and one was a close-up of Bríd's face. I remember thinking, Mick O'Dea has done what seemed impossible—he has managed to catch her face and above all those eyes.

That was more than confirmed later when I saw the portrait itself, hanging in the living room of Bríd and Micheal's house in Trimleston Avenue opposite another Mick O'Dea painting called "Bathed in Light," that is on the cover of Micheal's book about Bríd, *Love Life*. Even before that collection, in a poem that we will hear in a few minutes, Micheal used the phrase "That inward outward smile" about her face, and I think you can glimpse that in the portrait. The inward—Bríd's thoughtfulness, her inner poise, her memory for the important personal details; the outward—Bríd's compassionate seeing, alert to what is going on for the other person, silently asking you, "What do you need to tell me?" In the portrait, she could be just about to break into her smile; she might also be about to cry.

Then there is that hat, and the way she wears it. Just before I left to come over here from England my wife, Deborah, and I were reflecting on Bríd's elegance and breathtaking style. What flair she had! We recalled her shoes, her scarves, her skirts, her blouses, her coats, and so on and eventually came to the obvious conclusion: time and again, it was the whole outfit, everything together, her own fashion style. She once shared with me her collection of exquisite hat pins, showing them one by one. Deborah remembered how, on her last visit to us in Cambridge, she turned her need for support in walking into a fashion opportunity by leaning on a multicolored parasol. Her beauty and grace, too, were outward as well as inward.

She brought beauty to her home and garden. She was the main inspiration behind that wonderful collection of paintings and sculptures that fill the Trimleston home, together with innumerable other touches of elegance and daring combination. She loved cultivating plants too, and her garden has something of the style of her house and her clothes. I love Micheal's poem "Study" in *Love Life*, with its picture of two vocations in interplay. The first two parts of the poem are about his vocation as a poet. Then comes a sonnet that begins with Bríd seen in the garden below the study caring painstakingly for plants, a love she shared with her father.

> High in my dormer I see you hunching below
> To nurture a patch slowly made your own,
> Host to cuttings or shoots and happy although
> The garden you work is always a loan of a loan. . . .
> Your father in you stoops to hoe and weed,
> Fondles a shrub to know it grows and thrives,
> A guest tended and given pride of place
> As down by the Yellow River I strive to read
> My tortoise shells, and the seeds of invited lives
> Now breed in us worlds we bend to embrace.[1]

Micheal hunched over his writing, Bríd stooping over the garden—worlds we bend to embrace—and all in the language of hospitality: host to cuttings and shoots; a guest tended and given pride of place; the seeds of invited lives. I am sure many of us here today have enjoyed Micheal and Bríd's shared vocation of hospitality, those wonderful meals in Trimleston Avenue, or the parties, or book launches, or the welcome into conversations, or in recent years the small gatherings in Bríd's room in the Loyola wing of St. Mary's Centre.

But what was Bríd's vocation? What makes most sense of her life as a whole? Those are the questions that have gripped me most as I have wrestled in the past couple of days with the impossible task of trying to do justice to Bríd.

That care for plants and above all for people is a good part of it. She was a devoted daughter to both her father and mother—and her sister Áine describes their mother as "very loving, much like Bríd." In her many roles—sister to Áine, Anton, Francie and Pádraig, aunt to nephews and nieces, godmother several times over (including to a daughter of mine), friend and hostess to many of you here today—she showed the same loving attentiveness and thoughtful generosity. A present from Bríd was usually either just what you wanted or an imaginative gift you'd never dreamt of but that you fell for at once. She was always more interested in your life than in talking about herself.

For much of her adult life the two leading elements in her vocation were as a teacher and as Micheal's wife.

All the reports from colleagues and former pupils point to her as a superb and much-loved teacher. She had the gift of letting the children be themselves, with a sense of freedom and enjoyment, while at the same time knowing how to keep the order and discipline they needed to learn well. I like the story that she used to let them talk, play, and wander around the classroom until she tapped a ruler on her desk. One day a substitute teacher was trying in vain to control the class, raising her voice and threatening to no avail, until a little girl said, "This is how you do it miss," tapped a ruler on the desk, and the children immediately sat down and were quiet. It is no accident that she, like her brother Anton, eventually became a head teacher, and that the school flourished under her firm, gentle leadership.

As Micheal's wife she became perhaps the most written-about woman on this island. I do not know of anything to compare with *Love Life*, a whole book of poems about the first three decades of their marriage. He wrote it just after Bríd had accompanied him through nearly five years of immersion in testimonies and other literature of the Holocaust in the course of writing *The Gossamer Wall: Poems in Witness to the Holocaust*. She was reading those poems as they were written. We should not underestimate her formative role in this and other volumes of Micheal's poetry year after year. I have had the privilege of being the other first reader of his poetry alongside Bríd (just as he has for over four decades been the first reader of my theology). I know how much reliance Micheal has placed on the discernment and judgment of Bríd: he never published any poem that she had reservations about. *Love Life* was by far the most difficult of all his collections for her, and I think we owe her an immense debt of gratitude for allowing it to be published. It has been, I think, their most generous act of joint hospitality, welcoming us into their marriage, with its passions, routines, heights, depths, rows, and intimacies. *Love Life* has deservedly sold out, but thank goodness we will soon have it back in print, together with all the rest of Micheal's poetry about Bríd, and other topics, when his *Collected Poems* are published this September.

But if I were to choose just one of Micheal's poems about Bríd, I would go to another remarkable collection, *Our Double Time*. In that work, Micheal wrestled at length with dying and death, and then concluded with a section that has poems about some of those to whom he has been closest. The first person is Bríd. "Matins for You" is my favorite of all love poems. Here it is—here is Bríd:

> Come again glistening from your morning shower
> Half-coquettishly you'll throw
> Your robe at me calling out "Hello! Hello!"
> I turn over stretching out to snatch
> A bundle from the air and once more to watch
> That parade across your bower.

Jaunty, brisk, allegro,
Preparing improvisations of yet another day
As on our first morning twenty-seven years ago.

Sit on the bed-end and pull a stocking on,
Slip that frock over your head
Let it slither a little, ride your hips, then spread
Its folds and tumbles, flopping past those thighs
To swish against your ankles. I'm still all eyes.
The thrill and first frisson
At the half-known but unsaid,
At hints and contours embodied in a dance of dress
I'm ogling snugly from this your still warm bed.

Now you're hurrying, business-like and ready to go.
I wonder if I've ever glimpsed you
Or if all those years I even as much as knew
Behind those hints and suggestions I admire
What inmost aim or dream or heart's desire
Calls out "Hello, Hello!"
Flirt and peekaboo
Of such unwitting closeness, our take-for-grantedness,
Complex web of intimacies where we slowly grew.

Sometimes wells of aloneness seem almost to imbue
Your silence with the long wistful rubato
Of a Chopin nocturne or is it a seannós tremolo?
"Má bhíonn tú liom bí liom, gach orlach de do chroí
If you're mine be mine, each inch of your heart for me"
That infinite longing in you
A girl racing to follow
The bus's headlamps to meet your father at Bunbeg.
He steps down from the platform. Hello! Hello!

You smile your father's inward Zen-like smile.
And yet its light shines outward
As when I watched you helping a child to word
The coy, swaggering pleasure of new shoes,

204

A muse the more a muse in being a muse.
That inward outward smile
Delights in delight conferred,
Fine-tuning those strains and riffs of wishes unspoken,
Desires another's heart doesn't yet know it has heard.

Now I see you, now I don't. The doubt
And loneness of what's always new,
Moments seized in double time, love's impromptu,
As when late last night you started telling me
How even as a girl you'd known your dream would be
Bringing others' dreams about.
This once I think I glimpsed you,
You my glistening, lonely, giving Mistress Zen.
Thank you. Thank you for so many dreams come true.[2]

I think the heart of that poem is in the lines:

"*Má bhíonn tú liom bí liom, gach orlach de do chroí*
If you're mine be mine, each inch of your heart for me"

That is the language of their love.

"Matins for You" also throws more light on Bríd's vocation: she delights in delight conferred, and her dream is bringing others' dreams about. This is a vocation of being for others—while yet being utterly herself in how she dressed, spoke, smiled, and lived. Bríd had a vocation of love.

●　●　●

I am reminded of that passage in the autobiography of someone whom Bríd loved dearly, St. Thérèse of Lisieux, where Thérèse tells of her discovery of her vocation. It is significant in itself that she was wrestling with it even when she was already a Carmelite nun, which most would have called her vocation. She wrote that "I feel within me other vocations. I feel the vocation of the WARRIOR, THE PRIEST, THE APOSTLE, THE

DOCTOR, THE MARTYR. Finally, I feel the need and the desire of carrying out the most heroic deeds for You, O Jesus. I feel within my soul the courage of the Crusader, the Papal Guard, and I would want to die on the field of battle in defense of the Church."[3] But, as she meditated on these, she read Paul's first letter to the Corinthians, chapters 12–13, and the realization came:

> I understood that LOVE COMPRISED ALL VOCATIONS, THAT LOVE WAS EVERYTHING, THAT IT EMBRACED ALL TIMES AND PLACES . . . IN A WORD, THAT IT WAS ETERNAL!
>
> Then, in the excess of my delirious joy, I cried out: O Jesus, my Love . . . my vocation, at last I have found it . . . MY VOCA-TION IS LOVE![4]

As I try to see the last couple of years of Bríd's life in the light of her vocation of love, I think their importance goes beyond her roles as daughter, sister, aunt, godmother, friend, hostess, teacher, and even wife. Something remarkable was going on in St. Mary's Centre. It is very hard to put into words, and I have only seen parts of it. But here is a beginning attempt.

Her Parkinson's was first diagnosed over twenty years ago, and as it progressed it took away what I have been describing as elements of her vocation. First, she had to take early retirement from teaching, and, as time went on, her care of the house and garden, and her ability to be hostess, or to travel to see people, were affected. Then she had to go into care, leaving her home and marriage bed, no longer able to be Micheal's "bed and boarder" or first reader, and slowly she became almost completely dependent on other people for mobility and personal functions.

But here comes the mystery. I see three interwoven strands in it.

First, something like a new little community formed around her of those friends and relatives who visited her regularly. Bríd had not seen nearly as much of them before she went into care, but now they got far closer. And it was completely mutual—many have said that they always came out feeling the better for being with her, and she herself was greatly encouraged by the visits.

Second, there was St. Mary's Centre and the Loyola Nursing Home in particular. This larger community of residents, staff, and nuns welcomed her warmly, and she—and Micheal too—became fully part of it. Again, it was by no means one-way: Loyola was a gift to her, but she was also a gift to Loyola, and I have been very moved by the testimonies to this that I have heard in the past few days. And this was a worship-centered community—as Fr. Joe Dargan said yesterday, her faith deepened during this time, and the regular worship meant a great deal to both her and Micheal. Her vocation of love was grounded in trusting that she was—and is, and always will be—loved by God.

Third, there was her marriage. I have only glimpsed the depth and intensity of engagement between Bríd and Micheal during recent months. It has been inseparable from suffering on both sides, but it has been a witness to what we have just heard from the *Song of Solomon*: **Many waters cannot quench love, neither can floods drown it.** As a now somewhat lonely first reader, the decades of sharing the task with Bríd having ended, I have had the extraordinary experience of reading the poetry, still of necessity unpublished, that Micheal has been writing in the midst of all this. It is his most moving love poetry of all.

The main thing that strikes me about those three strands is that they are each about the community of the weaker and the stronger, and that they are also fully mutual. It's not about the strong condescending to do good to the weak. In each case, a richer, deeper love has come into being, centered on fragility, vulnerability, and what St. Thérèse would have called littleness.

207

Whether you are categorized as weaker or stronger is no longer what matters most: what really matters is loving and being loved.

I think Bríd has fulfilled her vocation of love in a way that is an encouragement to all of us, whether we are weaker or stronger, whether we are more like Bríd the head teacher or like Bríd the utterly dependent Parkinson's resident in St. Mary's Centre. But beyond that, I see her and those around her as a prophetic sign for a culture that far too often idolizes forms of independence, strength, success, wealth, and ability that have very little to do with sharing in community with those who lack those things— the dependent, the weak, the failures, the poor, and the disabled. But thank God for those of you who have resisted those idolatries and have instead—whether consciously or not—served the God who is love by being part of those circles of love around Bríd.

● ● ●

In conclusion, I return to Mick O'Dea's portrait of Bríd that you have in front of you. Micheal has given me permission to recite one of the many unpublished poems that he has written for and to Bríd since she has been in care, and which he was never able to share with her. When I retrieved it from my computer and read it out to him yesterday, he had forgotten the details of this one but agreed that it is appropriate. In it he speaks not only of Bríd choosing that red necklace she is wearing in the portrait but also of her deciding on the royal blue blouse in which she is now dressed in her coffin here before us—she chose what to wear today long in advance. The poem has no title—it is number ninety-seven in a sequence of sonnets called *One Crimson Thread*.

### 97

You pick red beads you got from Singapore
And tell me they're the keepsake kept for me;

You know I love that necklace that you wore
The day you sat for painter Mick O'Dea.
My darling red, your favoured royal blue,
The colour of the blouse you want to wear
Laid out; but less a realist than you,
Such down-to-earthness I'm not sure I dare.
We cannot plan who's first to go, I plead,
But lack of daring blinks at your ordeal;
So many signs I need to hear and heed.
"Does no one know," you ask, "how tired I feel?"
And either way a farewell both must face.
I fold you in another fond embrace.[5]

Let us have a moment of silence as we give thanks for Bríd and remember who she was and is for each of us.

Fr. Cormac will now lead us in the prayers of commendation.

# Notes

## Introduction

1. Micheal O'Siadhail, *Collected Poems* (Tarset: Bloodaxe, 2013).
2. David F. Ford and Frances M. Young, *Meaning and Truth in 2 Corinthians* (London: SPCK, 1987; Grand Rapids: Eerdmans, 1988; repr., Eugene, OR: Wipf & Stock, 2008).
3. This has also been true of his published work, though recently in prose he, too, has written of his side of the friendship—see "Facing Each Other: Friendship, Meaning, and Shaping a World," in *The Vocation of Theology Today,* ed. Tom Greggs, Rachel Muers, and Simeon Zahl (Eugene, OR: Cascade Books, 2013), 359–73.

## Chapter 1

1. O'Siadhail, "Traces," *Poems* (Tarset: Bloodaxe, 1999), 570.
2. O'Siadhail, "Crying Out," *Poems,* 619–21.
3. O'Siadhail, "Traces," *Poems,* 570.
4. O'Siadhail, "Echo-sounder," *Poems,* 494.

## Chapter 2

1. Ellen F. Davis, *Proverbs, Ecclesiastes, and the Song of Songs* (Louisville: Westminster John Knox, 2000).
2. O'Siadhail, "Study," *Poems,* 501–2.
3. See www.scripturalreasoning.org and www.interfaith.cam.ac.uk. Many of the themes of the present book are picked up by Mike Higton and Rachel Muers, *The Text in Play: Experiments in Reading Scripture* (Eugene, OR: Cascade Books, 2012).
4. For more on this see David F. Ford, "Scriptural Reasoning and the Legacy of Vatican II: Their Mutual Engagement and Significance," in David F. Ford and

211

Frances Clemson, *Interreligious Reading after Vatican II: Scriptural Reasoning, Comparative Theology and Receptive Ecumenism* (Malden, MA: Wiley Blackwell, 2013).

5. Sharon Ringe, *Wisdom's Friends: Community and Christology in the Fourth Gospel* (Louisville: Westminster John Knox, 1999).

## Chapter 3

1. O'Siadhail, "Transit," *Poems*, 267.
2. J. P. Stern, *On Realism* (London: Routledge and Kegan Paul, 1973).
3. O'Siadhail, "Middle Distance," *Globe* (Tarset: Bloodaxe, 2007), 20.
4. O'Siadhail, "Après Vous Monsieur!," *Poems*, 573–4.
5. O'Siadhail, "Between," *Poems*, 262.
6. Frances M. Young and David F. Ford, *Meaning and Truth in 2 Corinthians*, (Grand Rapids: Eerdmans 1988; repr. Eugene, OR, Wipf & Stock, 2008).
7. Frances M. Young, *Face to Face: A Narrative Essay in the Theology of Suffering* (London: T&T Clark, 1994).
8. David Ford, *Self and Salvation: Being Transformed* (Cambridge: Cambridge University Press, 1999).
9. O'Siadhail, "Cue," *Globe*, 40.
10. The best way into what L'Arche is about is probably through Vanier's writings, especially *Community and Growth*, 3rd ed. (London: Darton, Longman & Todd, 2007); a good anthology is in *Jean Vanier: Essential Writings*, selected with an introduction by Carolyn Whitney-Brown (London: Darton, Longman & Todd, 2008); there is also a fine biography: Kathryn Spink, *The Miracle, the Message, the Story: Jean Vanier and L'Arche* (London: Darton, Longman & Todd, 2006).
11. Jean Vanier, *Drawn into the Mystery of Jesus through the Gospel of John* (London: Darton, Longman & Todd, 2004).
12. David F. Ford, "An Interpersonal Wisdom: L'Arche, Learning Disability and the Gospel of John," in *Christian Wisdom: Desiring God and Learning in Love* (Cambridge: Cambridge University Press, 2007), 350–79.
13. Vanier, *Drawn into the Mystery*, 52, 55.
14. Ibid., 102, 105, 106.
15. O'Siadhail, "Admiral of Arks," *Poems*, 579–81.
16. Vanier, *Drawn into the Mystery*, 223.
17. Ibid., 227.
18. Ibid., 231–32.
19. Ibid., 173.
20. Ibid., 226.

## Chapter 4

1. O'Siadhail, "Duration," *Poems*, 538–40.
2. O'Siadhail, "Orchard," *Poems*, 334–35.
3. O'Siadhail, "Rehearsals," *Poems*, 328.
4. O'Siadhail, *Our Double Time* (Tarset: Bloodaxe, 1998), 30. The middle sonnets are in italics in the original.

5. See chapter 2 above.
6. Paul J. Griffiths, *Religious Reading: The Place of Reading in the Practice of Religion* (Oxford and New York: Oxford University Press, 1999), ix–x.
7. David F. Ford, *The Shape of Living: Spiritual Directions for Everyday Life*, 2nd ed. (Grand Rapids: Baker Books, 2004), 110.
8. O'Siadhail, "Hand," unpublished. Reproduced with permission.

## Chapter 5

1. O'Siadhail, "For My Friends," *Poems*, 179.
2. O'Siadhail, "Overflow," *Poems*, 375–76.
3. O'Siadhail, "Matins for You," *Poems*, 377–78.
4. O'Siadhail, "Secrets of Assisi," *Poems*, 378–80.
5. O'Siadhail, "Northway," *Poems*, 381–82.
6. O'Siadhail, "Oak," *Poems*, 384–85.
7. O'Siadhail, "Widening," *Poems*, 386.
8. Ibid.
9. O'Siadhail, "Our Double Time," *Poems*, 390.
10. O'Siadhail, "Homing," *Poems*, 475–76.
11. O'Siadhail, "Long Song," *Poems*, 476.
12. O'Siadhail, "For Real," *Poems*, 477.
13. O'Siadhail, "Exposé," *Poems*, 480–81.
14. O'Siadhail, "Sun," *Poems*, 479.
15. O'Siadhail, "Wobble," *Poems*, 486.
16. O'Siadhail, "Play," *Poems*, 488–89.
17. The names of groups on the model of Alcoholics Anonymous give some idea of common addictions: Anorexics and Bulimics, Cocaine, Clutterers, Crystal Meth, Codependents, CoSex and Love Addicts, Debtors, Food Addicts, Gamblers, Heroin, Marijuana, Narcotics, Neurotics, Nicotine, Overeaters, Online Gamers, Pills, Sexaholics, Sexual Compulsives, and Workaholics Anonymous. See chapter 6 for the Twelve Step Program that most of them follow.
18. O'Siadhail, "Faces," *Poems*, 468.
19. O'Siadhail, "Never," *Poems*, 467.
20. O'Siadhail, "Filling In," *Poems*, 484–85.
21. O'Siadhail, "Covenant," *Poems*, 490.
22. O'Siadhail, "Knot," *Poems*, 491.
23. O'Siadhail, "Clusters," *Poems*, 633–34.
24. O'Siadhail, "Giant," *Globe*, 626–27.
25. O'Siadhail, "Humbaba," *Globe*, 628–29.
26. O'Siadhail, "Accelerando," *Poems*, 626.
27. *Story of a Soul: The Autobiography of St. Thérèse of Lisieux*, trans. John Clarke (Washington, DC: ICS Publications, 1976), 192.
28. Ibid., 194.
29. Ibid., 197.
30. Ibid., 200.
31. On Arthur see Frances M. Young, *God's Presence: A Contemporary Recapitulation of Early Christianity* (Cambridge: Cambridge University Press, 2013),

*passim.* Frances Young has another book in preparation solely on Arthur, bringing his story up to date, to be titled *Arthur's Call.*

32. John Vanier, *Drawn into the Mystery of Jesus through the Gospel of John* (Toronto: Novalis, 2004), 298–99.

33. Adele Reinhartz, *Befriending the Beloved Disciple: A Jewish Reading of the Gospel of John* (New York and London: Continuum, 2001).

34. Ibid., 159.

35. O'Siadhail, "Session," *Poems,* 639–40.

## Chapter 6

1. O'Siadhail, "Mother," *Poems,* 664.

2. O'Siadhail, "Conditional," *Poems,* 698.

3. O'Siadhail, "Infinitive," *Poems,* 708.

4. Iain McGilchrist, *The Master and His Emissary: The Divided Brain and the Making of the Western World* (New Haven and London: Yale University Press, 2009).

5. O'Siadhail, "Cataclysm," *Poems,* 394.

6. O'Siadhail, "Entrance," *Poems,* 404–6.

7. For an interpretation of the Twelve Steps in line with this chapter, see Richard Rohr, *Breathing under Water: Spirituality and the Twelve Steps* (Cincinnati: St. Anthony Messenger Press, 2011).

8. O'Siadhail, "Vignettes," *Poems,* 408–9.

9. O'Siadhail, "Brink," *Poems,* 409.

10. O'Siadhail, "Chinks," *Poems,* 438.

11. O'Siadhail, "Blumenfrucht," *Poems,* 441.

12. O'Siadhail, "Recording," *Poems,* 443.

13. O'Siadhail, "Pastor Trocmé," *Poems,* 449.

14. Murray Cox and Alice Theilgaard, *Shakespeare as Prompter: The Amending Imagination and the Therapeutic Process* (London and Bristol, PA: Jessica Kingsley, 1994).

15. Ibid., 3.

16. Ibid., 193–94.

17. *The Independent,* August 30, 1997.

18. Margie Tolstoy, personal conversation.

19. O'Siadhail, "Tapestry," *Poems,* 346–47.

20. O'Siadhail, "Parkinson's," *Poems,* 532–33.

21. Soon after this was written, Bríd O'Siadhail died. A portrait of her, together with my funeral address, is in the appendix to this book.

22. Sue Morgan in one of her sessions at the L'Arche retreat.

23. Daniel W. Hardy with Deborah Hardy Ford, Peter Ochs, and David F. Ford, *Wording a Radiance: Parting Conversations on God and the Church* (London: SCM, 2010).

24. O'Siadhail, "Trace," *Poems,* 354.

25. O'Siadhail, "Whatever Else," *Poems,* 338–39.

26. O'Siadhail, "What If?," *Poems,* 337–38.

27. Hardy et al., *Wording a Radiance,* 144–45.

28. Ibid., 147–48.

29. Ibid., 137.

30. O'Siadhail, "Three Wishes," *Poems*, 340–41.

31. Words he used when reflecting on another of Micheal O'Siadhail's poems, "Autumn Report": *Even in this fall, wholehearted life reverberates / some almighty gaiety, invites me to adore / the immense integrity . . . I've never felt so near the centre / of all that is . . . Why hedge our bets / or play too cool? Detached we might miss / the passion to broaden the bore, deepen the joy.* O'Siadhail, *Poems*, 187–88.

32. O'Siadhail, *Our Double Time*, 94.

33. Hardy et al., *Wording a Radiance*, 149–50.

34. David F. Ford, *Christian Wisdom: Desiring God and Learning in Love* (Cambridge: Cambridge University Press, 2007).

35. Daniel W. Hardy and David F. Ford, *Living in Praise: Worshipping and Knowing God* (London: Darton, Longman & Todd, 2005). This is the second, revised edition of *Jubilate: Theology in Praise* (1984); *Praising and Knowing God* US edition (Philadelphia: Westminster Press, 1985).

36. Hardy et al., *Wording a Radiance*, 1–2.

37. Ibid., 12–13.

38. O'Siadhail, "That in the End," *Poems*, 370.

## Chapter 7

1. O'Siadhail, "Only End," *Poems*, 641–42. I have numbered the stanzas for ease of reference.

2. For these themes in some of his earlier poetry, see the final chapter of Ford, *The Shape of Living: Spiritual Directions for Everyday Life*, 2nd ed. (Grand Rapids, Baker Books, 2004), titled "Kaleidoscope—Resurrection, Joy and Feasting," which also relates him to Dante on heaven. The culminating poem quoted is the final poem of *A Fragile City*, "Dance," which is well worth reading alongside "Only End."

3. Dorothy L. Sayers, "'. . . And Telling You a Story': A Note on the *Divine Comedy*," in *Essays Presented to Charles Williams*, ed. C. S. Lewis (Grand Rapids: Eerdmans, 1966), 32.

4. Over many years of friendship with Jeremy Begbie, he has slowly educated me in the immense theological potential of music. His most recent work is *Music, Modernity, and God: Essays in Listening* (Oxford: Oxford University Press, 2013).

5. R. Kendall Soulen, *The Divine Name(s) and the Holy Trinity*, vol. 1, *Distinguishing the Voices* (Louisville: Westminster John Knox, 2011).

6. For my own brief account, see David F. Ford, *Theology: A Very Short Introduction*, 2nd ed. (Oxford: Oxford University Press, 2013). Of special relevance to the present section are chapter 3, "Thinking of God"; chapter 4, "Living before God: Worship and Ethics"; chapter 6, "Jesus Christ"; and chapter 9, "Experience, Knowledge, and Wisdom." Chapter 9 in particular expands on the question of what it means to know God, which complements what is said in this chapter.

7. Janet Martin Soskice, "Can a Feminist Call God Father?," in Teresa Elwes, ed., *Women's Voices: Essays in Contemporary Feminist Theology* (London: Marshall Pickering, 1992).

8. Soulen, *Divine Name(s)*, 249–50.

9. O'Siadhail, *Tongues*, in *Poems*, 795.

## Appendix

1. O'Siadhail, "Study," *Poems*, 501–2.
2. O'Siadhail, "Matins for You," *Poems*, 377–78.
3. *Story of a Soul: The Autobiography of St. Thérèse of Lisieux*, trans. John Clarke (Washington, DC: ICS Publications, 1976), 192.
4. Ibid., 194.
5. O'Saidhail, "97," *One Crimson Thread* (unpublished, 2013).